McCall's
How to Cope
with
Household
Disasters

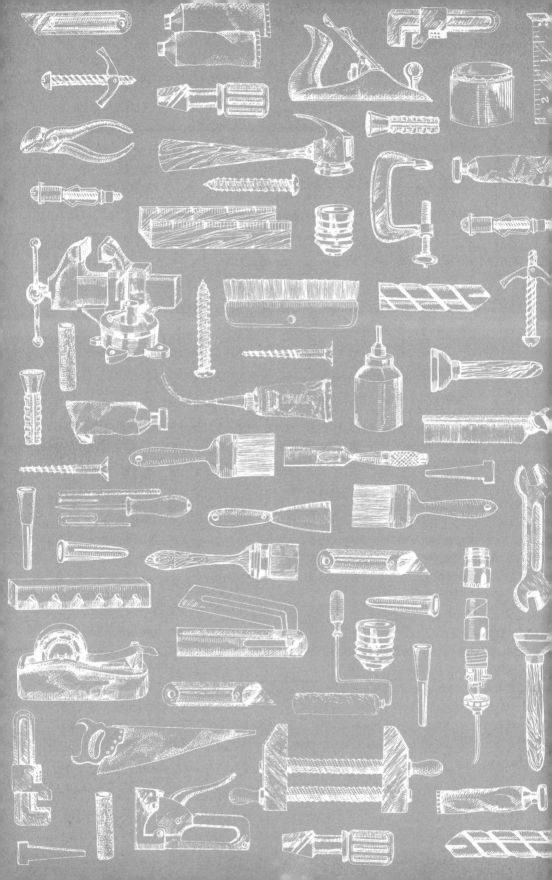

McCall's
How to Cope
with
Household
Disasters

Anna Fisher Rush
Home Management Editor of
McCall's

Illustrations by
Lilly Langotsky

Random House New York

The text of this book appeared in various articles in *McCall's*

Library of Congress Cataloging in Publication Data
Main entry under title:
McCall's how to cope with household disasters.
Includes index.
1. Repairing—Amateurs' manuals. I. McCall's magazine. II. Title: How to
cope with household disasters.
TT151.M25   643'.7   76-10647
ISBN 0-394-40775-X

Manufactured in the United States of America
24689753
First Edition

Contents

McCall's
How to Cope
with
Household
Disasters

Introduction

Repairman not available?
And you've got a clogged drain?
Quite a problem for the person who doesn't
have the know-how for repairs around the home.
We'll leave the hole in the roof
to the professionals,
but we'll tell you how to cope
with minor home
fix-it jobs,
the most common household problems
that you can
take care of yourself.
More than likely,
you'll save money on repairs,
and spare yourself a lot of frustration.

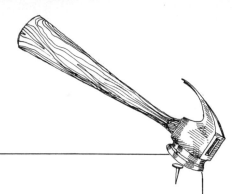

12 Tools
To Begin With

We begin with the basic tools that every person should have and know how to use. Organize them in a tool kit, something you can carry easily. It might be a ready-made tool caddie, a canvas bag, or a lunch box.

Screwdrivers

You'll need at least three sizes of the flat-blade type and two sizes of the phillips type. The phillips screwdriver has a crossed-blade point and is used for screws with a cross slot in the head. It is possible to purchase one screwdriver handle with an assortment of blades. To use a screwdriver, first bore a hole smaller in diameter than the screw with a hand drill. Apply the screw to the hole, tap it in place; and screw in with the correct screwdriver. If you don't have a drill, you can do about as well by driving a small nail into the spot where you want to insert the screw; then remove it carefully before putting in the screw.

Wrenches

One with an adjustable grip should be enough. Used for turning hexagonal or square nuts, the two jaws of the wrench span opposite sides of the nut, gripping it tightly when pressure is applied to the handle. To use, place the wrench on the head of the nut or bolt, so the force in turning the nut will be applied to the back of the handle. For loosening, reverse the procedure. Before turning, tighten the jaws so they won't slip. There are also socket wrenches, nonadjustable, each designed to fit a particular size of nut; they usually come in sets or kits with various sizes included.

Pliers

A gripper with metal teeth, pliers hold and tighten bolts, grip small rods, hold pipes, wooden pegs or studs, and bend wire. Pliers with a slip joint that allows the jaws to open wide at the hinge pin are the most useful kind. Some pliers double as wire cutters.

Cleanout Auger

Called a "snake," it's a long, flexible, steel cable that is run down drainpipes to break up obstructions and hook onto and pull out objects.

Hammer

Not just a plain hammer, this is a claw hammer. The curved claw at the opposite end of the face is used to remove nails. When pulling out a nail, place a small block of wood under the hammer so you don't mar the surface. To drive a nail, hold the handle near the end; use a wrist action for light blows, wrist and forearm for medium blows, arm and shoulder action with slight wrist movement for heavy blows.

Plunger

Commonly called a "plumber's friend," it's a rubber force cup with a handle. When a sink won't drain, pushing up and down with the plunger over the drain will force down or draw up small obstructions or foreign matter that may be clogging the drain. The cup over the drain, and enough water in the sink to cover the cup, plus the pumping action, clears the drain.

Adhesives

Glue, cement, mending and electrical tape: some adhesives are for specific jobs, some are all-purpose. Select an assortment for repairing luggage, household furnishings, plumbing and electrical fixtures, etc.

Nails, Screws, Nuts and Bolts, Washers

Have a good supply of these on hand, organized and separated. There are many sizes and types; consult your local hardware store for those most commonly needed and used around the home.

Hand Drill

Used to bore small holes in wood or metal before inserting screws. Drills generally come with bits of varying sizes for making different size holes. Select the correct bit, turn the drill's crank while applying pressure.

Electric Fuse

With extra fuses, plugs, sockets, and cords on hand, you'll be ready to change a fuse and repair lamps and other electrical appliances. We'll tell you how in future sections.

Measuring Rule or Tape

No handyperson should be without one. Choose either a rigid wood yardstick, a flexible metal tape, or a dressmaker's fabric measure, for exact measuring.

Utility Cutter

An all-purpose cutter with a razor-blade edge is used to open packages, cut tape, etc. It has a firm, safe, easy-to-manage handle for a good grip.

Besides the basic dozen, you'll also find useful: a flashlight; stapler (the kind that staples vertical surfaces); a small saw; lubricating oil; sandpaper of assorted grits; putty knife. Ask your hardware man for advice if you have special needs, but don't be overambitious. Handle the tools before purchasing, and choose ones of good quality that are comfortable for you to use. Remember: you don't need *every* tool. If you really need a plumber's size wrench, for instance, you'll probably also need the plumber.

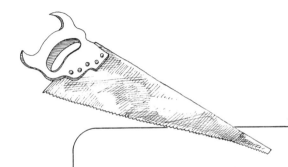

Special Tools For Special Jobs

Once you've mastered the simple repair jobs, it's time to progress to more complicated repairs and, thus, you'll need more complicated tools.

C-Clamps

There are many different kinds of clamps, but the one most frequently used is the C-clamp (named for its shape). It is used to apply maximum strength to glued joints while the glue is setting. Clamps also hold pieces temporarily in position while assembling joints with nails, screws or bolts, or hold adjoining members in accurate alignment when drilling holes. The C-clamp comes in a variety of sizes; two, with jaw openings of from three to six inches, are usually sufficient for most repairs.

Soldering Gun

This is a power tool that makes the joining of different metals quite simple and is also helpful for electrical repairs and for joining tubing. It has a pistol-shape grip and is operated by a trigger. The tip heats quickly, and the gun automatically turns off when trigger is released. Some units have replaceable tips so they can be used for purposes other than soldering.

Plane

Used for trimming and smoothing wood, planes are of various sizes and styles but all work generally on the same principle. The edge of the blade projects down through a slot in the tool's base. As the plane is pushed forward over a surface, the angled blade shaves off a layer of wood. The larger bench planes are more suitable for accurate trimming of long, straight pieces; smoothing rough lumber and fitting doors, for example. Smaller block planes, held with one hand, are convenient for working in tight corners and trimming around curves.

Staple Gun

A tool that drives staples into wood, the staple gun makes quick work of large jobs, such as carpeting floors or stairs, installing window screening, upholstering, etc. The tool is held firmly against the surface to be tacked; when the trigger is squeezed, a powerful spring drives the staple through the material and into the wood.

Miter Box

This is a simple, inexpensive tool used for guiding a handsaw at the proper angle when making a miter (or angle) joint in wood. A miter box aids in: cutting molding at a 45-degree angle with neat corners; cutting an angled wedge to be used as a brace on the underside of a chair; making notched blocks for reinforcement of table legs.

Electric Drill

One of the most useful tools to own, this bores holes in wood or metal and has a variety of special attachments, such as a masonry bit for plaster. Basically, drills are classified according to the size of the chuck (nose of the drill that opens and closes to accept various size bits). Either a $\frac{1}{4}$-inch or $\frac{3}{8}$-inch chuck is satisfactory for home use. The drill should be double insulated and have an adjusting trigger to turn it faster or slower (harder materials require slower drilling).

Bevel

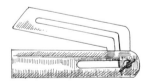

This is a tool used to draw angles to be given a bevel (the angle that one surface or line makes with another when they aren't at right angles). They come in various blade lengths and have handles of metal or wood.

Handsaw

There are two or three types that everyone should have. Perhaps you already have the basic crosscut saw, which is used for straight cuts across the grain of all types of wood. Available in various lengths, the most popular is the 24- or 26-inch model. A special type of crosscut saw is the backsaw; it has a spine of metal along the top and the handle is set at an angle to facilitate horizontal cuts. Often used with a miter box for accurate right-angle cutting, it has a fine-tooth blade that gives a smooth cut, with little or no sanding necessary. Another type, the hacksaw, cuts metal. It consists of a steel frame with replaceable blades that vary from 14 to 32 teeth to the inch, depending on the thickness and hardness of the metal. Most models are also adjustable to take either ten- or 12-inch blades.

Level

For checking the horizontal or vertical line of an item, a level usually has three vials. The bubble in a vial has to be between the two black lines on the side of that vial to mark an exact horizontal or vertical line. Levels are particularly useful for hanging shelves, installing paneling, and such.

Chisel

This is a finishing, cutting tool with a beveled edge, used to carve, cut or mortise. It's useful to have three: a $\frac{1}{4}$-inch and $\frac{3}{4}$-inch wood chisel and a ½-inch cold chisel (for cutting through masonry and metal). The standard chisel has a six-inch blade, but ones with shorter blades are available for working in tight corners.

Electric Sander

Finishing sanders are of two types: vibrator-driven units and motor-driven, or orbital, sanders. Intended for light-duty polishing and fine finishing, the vibrator unit moves the sandpaper with straight-line action. The motor-driven orbital sander is a heavy-duty machine that moves the sandpaper in a flat, oval path. It works faster than the vibrator type, can handle bigger jobs, costs a little more and is a good all-purpose machine. Some motor-driven models provide a choice of either straight-line or orbital action for various jobs by operating a key at the back.

Vise

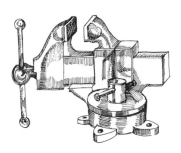

A holding device used to grip things as you work on them much like the C-clamp. It is made of heavy steel, with two jaws that can be adjusted by turning a handle. One type of vise is lined with wood to keep it from leaving any marks on the things it grips. Another type has metal jaws with sharp teeth; to avoid damage on delicate objects, lead or plastic inserts can be used to line the jaws. Or you can use this vise for woodwork without damage by sandwiching the work between two pieces of scrap wood.

Don't Get Stuck with the Wrong Glue

We've come a long way from the flour-and-water paste we once used to paste up our scrapbooks. The variety of glues available today makes it possible to mend almost everything, from furniture to pots and pans.

The selection of the right adhesive can be confusing. One important thing to remember is that no one product does everything. The trick is to know which glue is right for which surface; to know how much strength is required and whether your glue can provide it; and to know if your glue has the right characteristics (waterproof, heat resistant, quick setting, etc.) for the job. You may like the convenience of an electric glue gun. You may find that a spray adhesive will bond wall coverings or resilient floor tiles more quickly and conveniently. Read the package label carefully before you buy. Then stick to the following guidelines:

READ the instructions before using; follow them.

WORK in a well-ventilated area and, if possible, away from open flame.

CLEAN the surfaces to be joined; adhesives don't stick well to grease, dirt, rust, paint, or old glue.

ALLOW plenty of time to dry.

DON'T use too much glue.

Here are four basic types of adhesives that should be as common in the handyperson's toolbox as a hammer and a screwdriver.

White Glue

Vinyl base; milky white as applied, transparent when dry. Sets quickly; nontoxic; nonflammable; minimal pressure and clamping required; inexpensive; works best on porous materials, such as wood, paper, cloth, leather, cardboard, or cork. Not recommended for areas exposed to water, high humidity, or heat.

Use: Wood-furniture repair; wood veneer; pottery; hobbies; crafts.

Special directions: Roughen surfaces with emery board or sandpaper. Be sure glue penetrates cracks, crevices. Clamping provides a stronger bond.

Contact Cement

Provides immediate bond; requires no clamps; resists moisture and temperature extremes; is often flammable and toxic; therefore requires good ventilation; is inexpensive.

Use: Tile installation; paneling; felt work; luggage repair. Works well on wood, cloth, leather; most metals; some rubber and plastics; ceramics.

Special directions: Coat both surfaces, and allow to dry 15 to 30 minutes before joining. Align parts precisely as once surfaces touch they are impossible to adjust. Thorough drying may require 8 hours to several days.

Clear Cement

Dries colorless; resists water; works equally well with rigid or flexible joints; flammable; may be damaging to fabrics and finished surfaces if spilled; sets quickly but requires at least 24 hours to dry completely.

Use: Suitable for glass, china, ceramics, metal, leather, paper, wood; repairing dishes, leather luggage, belts, book bindings, costume jewelry.

Special directions: Nonporous surfaces should be roughened, joined pieces clamped while drying. Some cement will provide enough bond if held together about 20 seconds.

Epoxy Cement

Strongest; most expensive; waterproof; resists heat and shrinkage. Comes in two parts (adhesive and hardening agent); mix and use before it hardens.

Use: Will bond hard plastics, masonry, ceramics, metals, glass, pottery, porcelain, marble. Ideal for fastening fixtures to tiled walls.

Special directions: Thoroughly mix the adhesive and hardener, as directed. Some epoxy glues must be allowed to stand before application; others must be applied immediately but allowed to stand up to 15 minutes before surfaces can be joined.

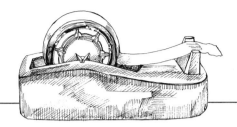

Picking the Right-Type Tape

Adhesive-backed tape can solve all sorts of household-repair problems—if you select the right one for the job. Household tapes generally fall into five categories: plastic, cloth, paper, glass-reinforced, and metal.

Cloth

Cloth adhesive tape has found its way out of the medicine cabinet and into the home-repair kit. It's generally less expensive than plastic tape and usually more resistant to rips and tears. Like plastic tape, it is available in a variety of colors.

Choose cloth tape for flat surfaces (plastic for uneven or curved surfaces). The double-faced version will secure rugs to a floor or fabric to a wall, is useful for patching children's clothes or work clothes, and will even fix a hem in an emergency.

Paper

The most familiar paperback adhesive tapes are masking tape and freezer tape. Masking tape, which comes in several widths, shields any adjacent surfaces—windows, baseboards—while you're painting. It enables a painter to keep colors separate in a two-color job. You can use it, as well, for wrapping and sealing packages that require extra-wide tape.

A new kind of masking tape is the paintstriper, used to paint decorative stripes on cabinets, picture mats, lampshades, and the like. The inch-wide tape is divided lengthwise into peel-away sections of three different widths. Lay the tape on the surface to be painted, press down, peel off the preferred-width strip, and paint the exposed area. Remove rest of tape just before paint is completely dry.

Freezer tape is masking tape made to withstand cold temperatures. Since it can be written on with a marking pen, it serves as both label and seal for freezer packages.

Plastic

Ever-faithful Scotch tape is the best known. It began a whole revolution in plastic tapes—and today they are stronger, clearer, and more versatile than ever. They come in a variety of bright colors, ranging in width from $\frac{1}{2}$ to $1\frac{1}{2}$ inches. Some are stretchable and ideal for repairing such things as shower curtains, patio cushions, and children's vinyl pools. There are even waterproof plastic tapes that seal leaks in garden hoses.

To remedy a draft around a window, weatherstrip the sash with 2-inch flexible foamed plastic tape. It has a smooth-surface finish and a quick-grabbing adhesive backing that keeps it firmly in place. This tape can also be used to wrap around cold-water lines to stop drips, or to cushion hand grips on tools.

Double-faced vinyl tape has lots of sticking power. Use it for mounting fabric on a wall, anchoring rugs and carpets, hanging pictures, laying tiles, or refastening loose wallpaper. It can be removed without leaving a trace of adhesive.

Electricians' tape may be of plastic, too. As with electrical tape of any material, be sure the one you select bears the UL (Underwriters' Laboratories) listed label that means it has been thoroughly safety-tested.

Metal

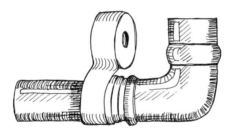

Aluminum-foil tape is ideal for patching leaky water pipes, pails and other pans. Generally in a 2-inch width, this tape is strong and forms a waterproof bond that makes it suitable for both outdoor and indoor use. Soft and pliable, it can be molded to curves or irregular shapes. It can mend gutters, patch downspouts, and also seal cracks and open areas around air conditioners installed in windows or walls.

Glass-Reinforced

A very strong tape, this has strands of glass fiber running through it. It's a sturdy sealer for large packages and heavy boxes when you're moving. It mends tool handles, reinforces flimsy containers. It comes in many widths.

A General Rule

Whatever tape you use, for whatever purpose, make sure the surface to which the tape is applied is thoroughly clean and free of moisture, dust, dirt, grease, and rust.

How To Control Skyrocketing Service and Repair Costs

Technology has been producing appliances that are easier to service and that require far less servicing; repair calls on automatic washers, for instance, have dropped 25 percent in the past ten years. Still, there are times when service is needed, and labor is costly. As you move farther out into the suburbs, it takes longer for a repairman to reach your home, which not only adds to the cost but creates scheduling problems. Satisfactory service depends on a number of factors, which we'll explore in this guide.

Consumer Responsibility

To avoid service calls, the consumer's responsibility begins when an appliance is purchased. Make sure the size of the washer, refrigerator or air conditioner is correct for present and future needs—undersized, overworked appliances can spell trouble. Learn appliance terminology: *i.e.,* the difference between self-cleaning and continuous-cleaning ovens, between automatic-defrosting and nonfrosting refrigerators. Make sure the appliance is properly installed—that the wiring is correct, the appliance is level and there is a sufficient supply of hot water for those appli-

21

ances requiring it. Read the instruction book *before* using the appliance to avoid errors. Make sure the appliance has a warranty, and read and understand its contents and terms. Finally, adopt a regular cleaning and maintenance program—check the instruction book for such things as cleaning of filters, and so on.

To Avoid Unnecessary Service Calls

About 40 percent of all service calls are unnecessary, wasting about $80,000,000 annually. You can avoid embarrassment and expense by checking the following before calling a service technician.

1. Make sure the appliance is plugged in.

2. Is the pilot light lit? Check owner's manual for lighting instructions.

3. Check the power source—a fuse may have blown or a circuit breaker been moved to the *off* position.

4. See that all controls are properly set. Consult owner's manual to be absolutely certain.

5. If lights are not on, check the power source. If bulb has burned out, the type of replacement bulb needed will be listed in the owner's manual.

6. Dust, dirt and lint can reduce efficiency. Dryer lint screens, air-conditioner filters and the coils on the back of or under refrigerators and freezers must be cleaned as directed in the owner's manual.

7. Be sure that water is flowing into an appliance, that faucets are turned on and hoses not kinked.

8. Check to see that doors and latches are closed properly—most appliances will not operate correctly unless these are tightly closed.

If, after making these basic checks and having checked the owner's manual, the appliance still does not operate properly, call the serviceman.

How to Locate a Serviceman

Don't call just any fix-it man down the street, and avoid do-it-yourself repairs that, if the appliance is still under warranty, could possibly void the benefits.

The owner's manual will frequently give very explicit instructions for obtaining service. In the case of housewares, a service-center listing is frequently packaged with the product. If your dealer does not have a service department, ask him to recommend an authorized service company. Some manufacturers have a toll-free line to corporate headquarters, from which you can get the name of the nearest service organization.

The Yellow Pages list service companies by product: *i.e.;* Ranges and Stoves—Repairing. In some areas the manufacturer may have his own service company, and this will generally be designated as factory service. Factory-authorized service means that the manufacturer has franchised or contracted an independent service agency to do the work for him. Periodic audits of service agencies assure high-quality service.

How to Report the Need for Service

When you call, be prepared to give the model and serial number and purchase date. State the problem, and if it's an emergency ask if there is anything you can do until the serviceman arrives. When setting up an appointment, tell them when you *will not* be home.

On the Day of the Service Call

Remove obstacles from the appliance to be serviced. Clean it so the serviceman can see where the problem is and what he's doing. Keep curious children out of the way. Have evidence of failure, such as a broken part or burned cake, on hand. Don't waste precious minutes talking while the man works—you're paying for his time.

If you're unhappy with the service you've received and are unable to resolve the problem locally, call or write the manufacturer, giving all the details (it would be helpful to tell him when you've had good service, too). If you are still not satisfied with the action taken, contact the Major Appliance Consumer Action Panel, 20 North Wacker Drive, Chicago, Illinois 60606. MACAP will take action on your problem and work toward its resolution.

Where Does the Service Dollar Go?

Because today's appliances are so complex, the skill to repair them has increased proportionately. Servicemen require advanced technical training. This level of competence commands a higher wage level over and above inflationary increases. Thus labor costs represent a major part of the service bill. Also inherent in the service charge is the larger parts inventory necessary to run an adequate service business because of more complex appliances. The cost of parts, if not covered by the warranty, is included in the bill.

Collection for repairs made on products that are out of warranty is quite diversified. Cash is the usual method of payment; most companies will accept a check, and some will accept a charge card or even bill you.

These days, warranties are written as briefly, clearly and simply as possible so that you know exactly what you are getting. However, there is no across-the-board rule for what is and what is not covered (parts and labor and for what period of time) and whether the warranty is transferable. It costs the manufacturer to fulfill the warranty terms and that cost is included in the price of the appliance, so you should be satisfied. When the warranty expires, you may wish to purchase a flat-fee service contract that gives another year's service.

When Your Drains Won't Drain

A clogged drain is more of a nuisance than a disaster, and one you can avoid with proper maintenance and periodic use of a drain cleaner. Always keep kitchen-sink drains free of grease and coffee grounds. Hardened grease and fat can catch coffee grounds, build up, and eventually block the drain. Don't let hair combings and lint accumulate in bathroom-washbasin drains.

But for all of your best efforts, sinks will clog. Here's what to do: First, make sure the problem is a local one. Check other sinks; if the kitchen sink is clogged, run water in the bathroom to see if drains work there. If all are stopped up, the problem could be at the main line, and for this you'll need a plumber. However, if only one drain is clogged, you can probably handle it yourself.

There's an interesting new tool on the market that may clear a drain in one simple operation. It's a $4.95 rubber device that connects to a garden hose. Placed in the drain, it expands to form a seal when the faucet is turned on. A surge valve sends powerful water impulses through the pipes that will loosen and clear the blockage. When the faucet is turned off, the device returns to its original shape and can be easily removed.

Otherwise, rely on the simple, standard tools that every household should have on hand: a rubber force cup with wooden handle, also called a plunger or plumber's friend; a metal drain auger, also called a snake (a wire hook made from a clothes hanger can sometimes do the job); and a wrench.

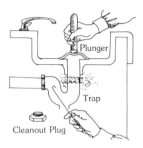

First, remove built-in drain stopper (turn counterclockwise, and lift). Clean out any tangled hair, bits of food, etc., that may be clogging the pipe or a lint trap, if there is one. If water still doesn't run out freely, the trouble is in the drainpipe or trap below the sink. Try the plunger first; it should be effective with slight stoppages. (If the sink is nearly full of water, bail most of it out, and dispose of it in a toilet or other unclogged drain, to prevent splashing as you work the plunger.) Leave enough water in the sink to cover the rubber portion of the plunger. It's good to plug the overflow opening (if there is one) with a wet rag, in order to get full suction and compression with the plunger. Position the rubber cup over the drain opening, and press the handle up and down in a jerking way, to create a suction action. This push-pull action should be repeated vigorously 10 times or more to dislodge foreign matter and break up stoppages.

If the plunger doesn't clear the drain, try a chemical drain-pipe cleaner. These cleaners are caustic and must be handled with care. If the sink is filled with water, bail it all out. Pour the compound directly into the drain opening, without letting it come into contact with sink finish. The amount of cleaner and time required for it to work will vary with the problem; two applications may be required. When the drain is open, flush it thoroughly with lots of cold water to clear the pipe of any remaining cleaner.

If this doesn't work, try the snake. Push it down the sink-drain opening, to clear the pipe down to the trap. If you still aren't getting anywhere, the stoppage is further on, and you must open the trap. (If you've used a chemical compound beforehand, wear rubber gloves, and don't let it get on your skin or in your eyes.) Place a pail or bowl beneath the trap to catch any waste water. If the trap has a cleanout plug, remove it with an adjustable wrench. (If no cleanout plug is provided, then remove the U-shape trap by unscrewing the nuts that hold it in place.) Clear out trap with the snake or a wire hook, and scrub with a bottlebrush. If the stoppage is in the drain line beyond, push the snake into the pipe. Twist the handle so that the hook or coiled spring at its tip hooks into the obstruction; break it up, or bring it back through the cleanout opening. Drain should be cleared by now. Replace all parts.

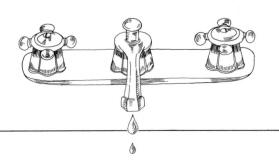

No More
Leaky Faucets

The steady dripping of a leaky faucet is annoying. It can also be expensive, especially if it's the hot-water tap. Faucet repair is extremely simple. All you need is a wrench, a screwdriver, and possibly a seat-dressing tool.

Screw

Packing Nut

Handle

Valve Stem

Washer

Sealer

Screw

There are several reasons why a faucet may leak: (1) Faucet parts may be loose and simply need to be tightened; (2) packing around the valve stem may have deteriorated; (3) the valve washer may be worn out; or, (4) the valve seat may be nicked or pitted and need regrinding.

Most modern faucets have dual handles and a single spout, as shown in the illustration. The separate parts that fit into the handle assembly are shown also. (All of these parts may be obtained at plumbing and hardware stores.) Older faucets combine handle and spout in one unit, but they are similarly constructed and similarly repaired. (Our repair instructions do not apply to the new faucets that are controlled by a single lever; they are more complex and require the services of a plumber.)

1. If water is leaking from around the stem of the faucet just below the handle, first try tightening the packing nut (the hexagonal nut to which the handle is attached) with a wrench. Wrap cloth or friction tape around nut to protect its finish. Also check for loose exterior parts, such as the handle itself; tighten with wrench or screwdriver.

2. If this doesn't stop the drip, the packing under the nut may need to be replaced. First, shut off the water—either below the sink or at the main water-supply valve (it is wise for all members of the family to know the location of this main valve for emergency purposes). To remove the packing nut, first remove the faucet handle. If there is a sealer, remove it. The handle may be held on with a screw at the top, it may be covered with a cap or plate which snaps off or unscrews, or it may have a screw underneath the handle. Or, by loosening the packing nut and turning the faucet handle counterclockwise, the handle may be lifted from the body of the faucet. The packing nut can then be unscrewed and lifted from the faucet. Underneath, you will find the packing—graphite-impregnated, fibrous material—wrapped around the stem beneath the nut. If that looks frayed, raveled, or worn, replace it. You can buy packing at hardware stores. Some newer faucets may have a packing ring—a washerlike object—beneath the nut instead of the fibrous material. If this is worn, it can be replaced. In other faucets, the ring is contained in the nut, in which case the whole nut must be replaced.

3. If the faucet still drips, the washer at the lower end of the valve stem may be at fault. This washer is held in place by a brass

screw. Lift out the valve stem, remove the screw, pry out the old washer with the tip of a screwdriver, and insert a new one of the same size, thickness, and shape. You'll find an assortment of replacement screws and various sizes of faucet washers at the hardware store. You might as well also use a new brass screw. A snap-in type of replacement washer doesn't need a screw to hold it in place.

4. The only remaining problem area is the valve seat, the opening beneath the valve stem. The washer fits into it. If there are nicks or scratches in the valve seat, the washer won't fit tightly, and the faucet will leak. Remove the valve stem and washer, and check the condition of the valve seat with your finger or with a flashlight. If it is damaged, it can be reground. Most hardware stores sell an inexpensive seat-dressing tool. It has a threaded spindle with handle attached and a hard-steel cutting disk at the bottom. The spindle fits into the faucet, in place of the stem, centering the cutting disk on the middle of the faucet seat; just a few turns of the handle smooth the faucet seat clean. Flush out any metal particles with water before reinserting the faucet stem.

Some faucets have a renewable valve seat. If this is the case, remove the valve seat, and replace it. In other faucets, the seat is part of the valve stem, in one piece, and you must replace the entire valve stem with the same type.

After repairing your faucet, be sure to replace all parts in the proper order and then tighten the packing nut and the top screw that holds the handle. Otherwise, the dripping will start all over again.

Thumping, vibrating noises in faucets are usually caused by worn parts, and the above directions could apply. This hammering sound might also occur when water is brought to a sudden stop. Too much water pressure is usually the cause. You can check with your water company to learn what the pressure is in your area. If it exceeds 40 to 50 pounds per square inch (considered normal), a pressure regulator might be the solution.

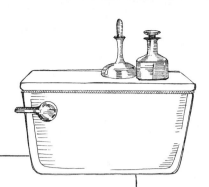

Toilet Tank
Fix-its

The frustration associated with toilet-tank disorders can be traumatic. However, you can handle the breakdowns of a toilet quite easily if you will learn a little about the mechanism within the tank. Water closets may vary somewhat in the design of the flushing mechanism, but they are similar enough so that general repair instructions are possible.

The parts most often in need of repair are the FLUSH VALVE, the INTAKE or FLOAT VALVE, and the FLOAT BALL.

If the water runs but the tank doesn't fill, the first thing to check is the flush valve. When the rubber ball of this valve becomes soft or out of shape, it won't sit properly, which causes the valve to leak. To install a new TANK BALL, unscrew the old one from the LIFT WIRE.

The lift wire or the TRIP LEVER may corrode and fail to work smoothly. Disassemble, clean each part with steel wool. Replace whatever is necessary.

The tank ball may be in good condition, but still isn't dropping onto the seat of the flush valve properly. In this case, loosen the screw holding the METAL GUIDE for the lift wire, and jiggle the guide back and forth so the ball will drop directly into the seat. Once it is reseated properly, tighten the guide screw. (While working on

31

the flush valve, the flow of water can be stopped by propping up the float ball with a piece of wood. Be careful not to bend the rod of the float ball out of alignment.)

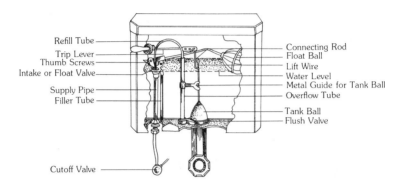

Convenient to have is a toilet-tank-repair kit called the "Silent John." It has a ballcock (consisting of supply pipe and intake or float valve), tank ball, float ball, lift wires, and float rods, and instructions. Costs about $6 at hardware and department stores. Individual parts are available at hardware and plumbing-supply stores.

If it's necessary to hold down the handle in order to flush the toilet, the problem may be a leaking intake or float valve. No doubt the plunger washer in the SUPPLY PIPE is worn. To replace the washer, shut off the water (at the CUTOFF VALVE), and drain the tank by flushing the toilet. Unscrew the THUMBSCREWS that hold the levers, and push the levers out. Lift out the plunger, unscrew the cup on the bottom, and insert a new washer. Check the REFILL TUBE to be sure it's bent to allow the water from it to go into the OVERFLOW TUBE. The refill tube is usually copper and bends easily. (Some new tubes may be plastic.) Check the handle on the tank. If it's loose, tighten by holding with one hand on the outside while turning the inside nut with a wrench.

Another possible problem: If the tank fills but the water continues to run, check the float ball. It may have developed a leak so that it cannot rise to its proper position. When this happens, the intake valve remains open and water continues to flow. If the float ball is submerged, with water covering more than half of it, the ball probably has a leak. Unscrew it, and shake to see if it contains water. If it does, get a new one. If this is not the problem, adjust the float arm by bending it slightly until the float is about one half inch lower than it was. The float arm should float high enough to stop the water flow about one half inch below the top of the overflow tube. If it doesn't, keep bending the float arm until it does.

If the tank "sweats," cold water entering the tank is chilling the tank enough to cause condensation of atmospheric moisture on the outer surface of the tank. A tempering device may be installed on the water-supply line, to warm the water before it enters the tank. Or try insulating liners from plumbing-supply or hardware stores. They fit inside the tank to keep the outer surface above the dew-point temperature of the surrounding air.

What to Do When the Lights Go Out

When lights go out mysteriously or an appliance slows down and quits on you, is your first thought to call an electrician or repairman? And hate yourself afterward when you get his bill for what turned out to be a very simple job? You can handle many household crises yourself, if you take time to learn how your wiring system works.

Most power problems are caused by overloaded circuits or short circuits. The first step in learning to solve these problems is to find out how your home is wired.

Electric power comes into your house to a distribution center. The power is then diverted into branch circuits that are totally independent of each other. Each circuit is equipped with a safety device—either a fuse, which will blow if there's trouble on the circuit, or, in newer houses, a circuit breaker (a switch that trips automatically). The box that holds the fuses or the circuit breakers is at the distribution center. This box can usually be found in the basement or the kitchen.

The number of fuses or circuit breakers in the box tells you the number of circuits you have. A small apartment may have four, a house may have ten or more. General-purpose circuits accommodate lights and a few appliances, such as clocks and radios. Circuits in the kitchen-dining-laundry area are geared to take a number of appliances operating simultaneously. Major appliances—electric range, dryer, dishwasher, air conditioner—have their own special circuits. You can tell which circuits serve which areas, generally, by turning on all the lights and removing the fuses, or tripping the circuit breakers, one by one. The area that blacks out is the area controlled by particular fuses or circuit breakers.

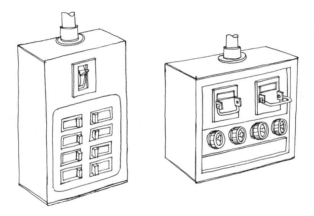

It's a prudent idea to make a map of your circuitry, with circuits marked for each area of the home and for individual appliances.

The most common problem is overload. If one fuse blows frequently, if the blender runs slowly, if the toaster doesn't heat up properly, or if the TV picture shrinks while you're ironing, you have too many appliances plugged in to the same circuit. The immediate solution is to unplug the extra appliances and reset the circuit breaker or replace the fuse. Then avoid plugging in too many appliances at one time. Heating appliances—toasters, coffee makers, skillets—are a big drain on the power. A safe rule of thumb is to not have more than one heating appliance or two motor-driven appliances operating on the same circuit at the same time.

The long-range solution—if you're inconvenienced by having to limit the use of appliances—is to rewire, adding additional circuits. Wiring that was once adequate may no longer be because of the many new electrical appliances that have been or are being added to today's homes. (Consult a licensed electrician about rewiring.)

If you've never changed a fuse: It's simple. Be sure to stand on a dry, insulated surface—if the basement floor is damp, stand on a board. Turn off the main switch, if you have one. Unscrew the dead fuse (usually it has a discolored window, or the metal strip is broken), and screw in a fresh one. Turn on the main switch. Don't use a fuse substitute or a fuse of higher amperage. Fifteen amperes is standard for most residential purposes; a 20-amp fuse or a penny may get all the appliances working again, but you run the danger of causing a serious fire. Don't forget, a fuse is essentially a safety device.

To reset an automatic circuit breaker that has tripped open: remove the source of the trouble; reset the switch by turning to the "on" position.

If you discover that overload isn't the problem, you may have a short circuit. A short circuit is an improper electrical connection between current-carrying wires or a current-carrying wire and a ground, and is caused usually by a faulty plug, wire, or appliance. To check this out: Turn off the main switch at the fuse box; connect all appliances and lamps to the outlets serviced by the problem circuit, but keep each appliance turned off. Remove the fuse for this circuit; insert a light bulb in its place. Turn on the main switch. If the bulb lights, it indicates a short. Unplug each lamp or appliance; when you have unplugged the lamp or appliance that's causing the trouble, the light bulb will go out.

If you have circuit breakers instead of fuses, unplug all the appliances and lamps, reset the circuit breaker, and plug them in again, one by one. The culprit will trip the circuit breaker. Don't use it again until it's repaired.

If the bulb in the fuse box stays lit after you've pulled out all the plugs, or if no lamp or appliance trips the circuit breaker, then there's a short in the circuit wiring. This is something you can't deal with, and you must call the local power company or a licensed electrician.

You may be in the dark when coping with many of these problems: the wise handyperson has a working flashlight in a familiar place to light the way.

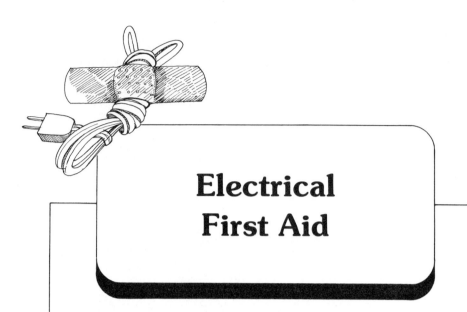

Electrical
First Aid

Major electrical repairs are best left to an electrician, but minor repairs can be made by the careful handyperson.

Plugs

If prongs are loose, badly bent, or corroded, or if the plug body is cracked or worn, the plug should be replaced. There are two common types: open construction and those that have the prongs sealed in composition or rubber. Use only the open-construction plug for replacements. (Many major appliances have a three-prong plug. McCALL's doesn't recommend repairing or replacing these.)

If a sealed plug is broken or cracked, cut it off, and discard it. (Use sharp scissors or a utility cutter, and if cord is frayed, cut off all the frayed part.) If only the cord attached to an open-construction plug needs repairing, and the plug itself is in good condition, you can use it again. After cutting the plug away from cord, remove the fiber disc, and note how the wires are fastened to the screws. Loosen screws, but don't remove. Pull wires out, and save the plug.

To Prepare Cord

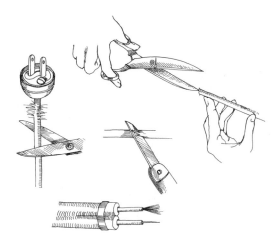

Using scissors or knife, remove fabric covering at end of cord; separate wires about two inches. If cord is of molded rubber, carefully cut or pull the wires apart, again about two inches. Pare away rubber insulation at the end of each wire, exposing about three-quarters of an inch. Do not cut strands of wire. Scrape wires clean with back of knife blade. Twist the strands of fine wire tightly together.

To Replace Attachment Plug

Bring the two prepared wires through the hole in back of the attachment plug. For fabric-covered cords, wrap a few turns of thread or black-friction tape around the end of the outside fabric. Tie the wires in an Underwriters' knot, see page 40. Pull knot back into the recess in the plug between the two prongs. Loop each wire clockwise around each prong, and wrap the exposed strands around terminal screw. Tighten screws, making sure no loose wires stick out. Replace fiber disc.

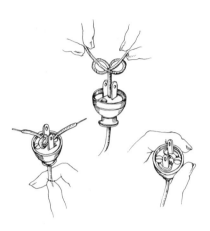

To Repair Appliance Plug

An appliance plug—the plug that plugs *into* the appliance—differs from an attachment plug in appearance, but repair procedures are similar: Disconnect cord; cut off plug and adjacent frayed cord. Take plug apart, and note the position of wires, clips, and terminals. Remove wire from terminals and coil spring guard; discard. If the body of the plug is in good condition, use it again. Put cord through spring guard. As with attachment plug, prepare ends of wire, tie Underwriters' knot, and attach wires to terminal clips. Reassemble plug by placing wires and clips in grooves in half of plug; replace cover and screws.

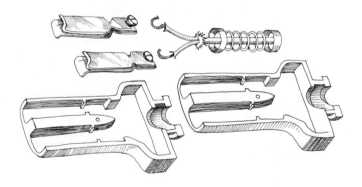

Cords

Service cords are of different types and construction. They're not interchangeable. Always replace a worn cord with the same type. If a break occurs too far away from the end to replace plug, a new cord should be used. Buy a cord with the UL listed label. McCall's does not recommend splicing service cords.

Take appliances with permanently attached cords to a service center for cord replacement.

Lamp Sockets

A defective lamp can be a fire hazard and should be repaired immediately. If cord and plug are in good condition, the problem is probably in the socket. Sockets are similar in construction; most have a brass shell, with cardboard lining and a built-in switch in the body (see illustration). Wire enters through cap at the bottom and is fastened to terminal screws inside the body.

Disconnect the lamp. Look for the word PRESS on the brass shell, and press hard while twisting the cap and pulling the shell off. The body can then be lifted off the cap. Check the connections where wires wrap around the terminal screws. If screws are loose or a wire has broken, the necessary repairs can be made and the socket reassembled. Otherwise, install a new one. Often, the original cap can be left in place and only a new body and shell installed. If cap must also be replaced, examine the construction of the lamp before taking it apart so that the parts can be properly replaced. To install new socket, wrap wires (repaired, if necessary, following previous directions) clockwise around the terminal screws. Press the shell, lining, and the body back into the cap.

Lighting Up In Safety

Holiday lighting decorations, from a simple tree of lights to an elaborate front-yard display, can be a glorious sight to remember—or the cause of a tragedy you'll never forget. Follow these simple rules to make your holiday season both festive and safe.

Outdoors

When working with outdoor wiring, be sure to turn off the electricity: the least bit of dampness combined with electricity could mean disaster.

For temporary wiring outside the house, use only outdoor extension cords (at least number 16 in size) with permanently molded plugs and sockets. Drape cords that run along the ground over Y-shaped wood spikes to keep the cords well above snow and slush. As an added precaution, wind insulated tape around each connection to keep it watertight. Cords that run in the eaves or along the side of a house can be kept in place with insulated staples or drive rings (purchased at the hardware store). If loose wires are blown about by high winds, their insulation *could* wear out from abrasion damage.

For extensive outdoor decorating, permanent underground wiring offers maximum safety and convenience. This installation is, however, a job for experts: call an electrical contractor, and have it done correctly.

Sockets, plugs, cords, and bulbs for outdoor lighting must be weatherproof. When you screw bulbs into sockets, use gaskets (round rubber rings); they prevent moisture from getting into sockets. Gaskets also seal sockets against bits of greenery. As a further precaution against moisture, hang sockets downward.

Lights, as opposed to some appliances, work efficiently on very low voltage. There is a low-voltage, outdoor wiring kit for spot-lights. It includes a transformer that reduces normal 115 to 120 voltage to 12 volts. There are many advantages: lower operating costs, easy installation, and a safe, low, yet completely efficient voltage.

For safety and beauty, figure the maximum number of lights to use on a tree by measuring the width of the tree, multiplying that by its height, then multiplying by three.

Indoors

When using indoor lights, be careful not to overload any circuits. Do *not* plug the lights into a circuit that is already burdened with lamps and appliances. This is especially important to remember if you're using several sets of lights on the tree and are decorating with other electrical ornaments. If the circuit won't take the extra lights, *don't* replace your own fuse with one of higher amperage. Fuses are safety devices. When they blow, it's a warning that the circuit is overloaded. If you use a 20-amp fuse in a circuit requiring a 15-amp, the lights will go on—but you will also run the risk of a fire. Before decorating, inspect previously used sets of lights for burned-out bulbs, frayed cords, exposed wire, and broken sockets. After years of use, some replacements may be necessary. When you're buying new strings of lights, make sure that they are UL (Underwriters' Laboratories) listed.

Drape wires on a tree so that lights fall between the branches, and not on them. Position the bulbs so that they touch the needles as little as possible. (Also, use a tree stand with a water container, and keep the container filled. This keeps the tree as fresh as possible.)

Be sure any artificial tree you buy is flame retardant; trees with built-in electrical systems should be UL listed. Floodlights and spotlights are safer and prettier for metallic trees than strings of lights.

Don't place indoor extension cords under rugs or in areas where you might trip over them.

Always disconnect lights when the family is asleep or away from the house.

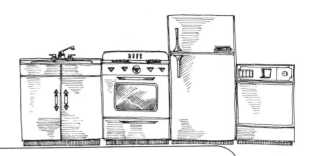

Preventive Medicine for Major Appliances

Someday someone will invent a home that is completely self-sufficient—the dishes will suds themselves, the rug will automatically shed assorted spills and crumbs, the refrigerator will keep itself sparkling clean. But for the time being, your home demands a certain amount of time and attention to keep it in tip-top shape. This program of care is called "preventive maintenance," and it does just that—prevents problems from occurring and extends the life of your appliances by keeping them in optimum working order at all times. Here are some timely tips to help you create a preventive maintenance program for your major appliances.

Your Range

To protect the beauty of the finish of your appliance, don't use harsh cleaners—in time they may age your porcelain enamel or metal trim. When your range is cool, clean the exterior surface with soap and water, or use a mild cleaner applied with a damp cloth. Occasionally, apply a thin coat of creamy cleaning wax over the finish—and don't slide pans across the top surface or ugly marks will appear (a range-protector pad is always a good idea).

Save your range from lackluster spots; wipe food spills up the moment they happen, especially if they're acidic in nature. If the spots tenaciously cling to the metal trim, rub with a mild abrasive cleanser; otherwise, a healthy dose of soapy water, followed by an immediate rinsing and drying, should eradicate the surface spills. Clean the control panel with a sudsy cloth, rinse and wipe dry. If the control knobs are removable, take them off occasionally to reach the grime underneath.

Remember to check those secret sections of your range (under the reflector pans and in and around the gas burners) where dirt and grime builds up. With some ranges it's easy to get at these areas—the whole cooktop just lifts up so that you can reach underneath.

If your range is not of this easy-to-care-for variety, you usually have the option of unplugging the surface units or lifting them to an upright position (make sure the units are cool before you handle them with naked fingers or a flammable cloth) in order to remove the metal trim and reflector pans. Wash them in warm sudsy water, but don't immerse them—a wipe with a damp cloth should be sufficient, as most real soil burns itself off in the cooking process.

Wipe gas burners after each round of heavy cooking to remove spill-over deposits and grease splatters before they have a chance to harden and crust on the surface. For a very thorough cleaning, the burners must be removed. Pay close attention to how they come out so that you'll be able to replace them later. Lift out grates and burner or aeration pans (on new ranges the entire cooktop can also be lifted) to expose the burners, then lift them out. Immerse burners in water containing detergent. For stubborn soil, mix one tablespoon baking soda with three quarts of hot water as a cleaning solution. Soap-filled steel-wool pads may also be used, but avoid scouring powder as it may clog ports further.

While burners are out and cooktop is in raised position, wipe out surface below burners where spillovers and dust may have collected. Dry burners thoroughly in warm oven before replacing. Check instruction booklet to make sure burners are replaced correctly and fit well.

Foil should not be used to cover up the openings of your reflector pans. If you must use foil, tightly mold it around the edges of reflector pans so that no open spaces are blocked. When molding foil to the contours of your broiler pan, secure it tightly around the edges of the broiler rack and slit the taut foil to conform to the slits in the rack; this allows the grease to drop through to the pan below and minimizes smoking and splattering.

If your oven is self-cleaning or continuous cleaning, never attack its interior surfaces with an oven cleaner. If you simply give the oven an energetic wipe after each use, real cleanings will be few and far between.

In the oven, the capillary tube with thermostat bulb at its end is not removable. This device senses oven temperatures and is a fragile part of the range; it shouldn't be kinked or broken. To clean, gently wipe it. It is especially wise to do this following the use of an oven cleaner, because if an accumulation of the cleaner builds up on the temperature bulb, an inaccurate control may result.

In many ovens, the shelf supports as well as the shelves are removeable; take them out periodically to get at all gritty, grimy places on the oven wall. Clean the supports and racks themselves in your sink with a mild abrasive cleaner.

Always remember: When in doubt about what can or can't be removed from your range, consult the finest possible authority— the instruction manual that accompanied your appliance, which should set you straight about taking off oven doors, the windows in these doors, top panels, shelf supports, etc.

If your oven door does have a window, clean it with a sudsy cloth or a mixture of ammonia and water but don't allow water to seep through and run into the inner part of the window. If you have stubborn stains use an ammonia solution. If the range is hooded, clean this section frequently by washing it with sudsy water both inside and out. If your hood has a charcoal filter, replace it once a year; if it has a permanent filter, remove it and soak the filter in sudsy water for a few minutes, then rinse and dry it carefully before setting it back into the hood.

Your Dishwasher

Avoid harsh cleaners that may leave scratches on the bright finish. Instead, wipe the surface with long strokes using a sudsy cloth and periodically use a cream cleaning wax. The interior of the dishwasher is usually self-cleaning. Occasionally, however, turn your attention to the inside door edges; wipe these clean with a sudsy cloth. If you live in a hard water area, a lime deposit may form a grayish film inside the dishwasher tub. To remedy this, try the following: Place two bowls of white vinegar on the bottom rack (don't add detergent); start the machine, and let it operate through the wash and rinse cycles; stop the machine after the final rinse and before the dry cycle begins. Remove the bowls and turn the dial back to the "start" position. Add dishwasher detergent and run the machine through a complete cycle.

Your Refrigerator

Just because your refrigerator may not need defrosting, don't think it doesn't have to be cleaned. When food is spilled, wipe it up immediately—otherwise odors will rise from the depths of your refrigerator to haunt you. In some models, spillage may cause clogs in the vital drain areas that carry the defrosted water away; if you let this happen, puddles will form.

Occasionally, give loving care by wiping the storage racks and the interior with a baking-soda solution (one tablespoon soda to one quart warm water). Include the door gasket (the pliable band around the edge of the door) in your cleaning regime, and don't forget the drawers, the condenser coils and the defrosting-water pan. This pan, located behind the base grille at the bottom of your appliance, should be washed at least once a year to prevent odors and assure the proper operation of your refrigerator.

Twice a year vacuum your refrigerator's condenser coils (they're located either on the back of the cabinet or behind the base grille) to suck up the dust and lint that lingers there (if not kept clean, the motor may not run properly). Rinse the refrigerator down with warm sudsy water, and obtain a fabulous finish with an occasional cream waxing of the exterior cabinet.

If your freezer's the type that requires defrosting, twice a year is the recommended interval for this task. Humidity, climate and amount of usage also play a large part in the timing. In between major defrostings, scrape off excess ice with a wooden spatula or plastic scraper. Never use an ice pick or any other sharp instrument!

Your Washer

One of the wonderful things about washers are that they require little or no washing themselves—the inside of the appliance keeps itself clean; the outside should be wiped only occasionally with a damp cloth (don't forget to wipe the inside of the lid). Keep your filter free of lint; if removable, run it under water now and then.

If you use your washing machine for something other than washing—dyeing or starching, for example—don't forget to rinse out the machine afterwards. An easy way to accomplish this is to add less than the normal amount of detergent to your washer and run the appliance through a complete cycle.

Your Dryer

The exteriors of dryers and washers share the same basic requirements for a preventive-maintenance regime. For dryer interiors, wipe the drum with a damp cloth after drying newly starched or dyed items.

Clean out the lint filter after each load to prevent any buildup of the lint which will ultimately decrease the efficiency of the filter. Never operate your dryer without this filter in place, but if it is removable, take it out occasionally and clean the opening with a vacuum cleaner.

Your Air Conditioner

The secret to maintaining an air conditioner is in the care of the filter. Be it permanent or replaceable, clean it out so as not to hamper the passage of air. Dirty filters not only hinder the distribution of air and its cooling properties, but they cause the waste of fuel and money. Check the filter frequently; the cleaner it is, the more efficient the operation.

Most filters are easily accessible; check your instruction booklet to find out where exactly the filter is located on your appliance and what category it falls into. If it's the permanent type, remove, clean and return it; if it's replaceable, remove it and replace it at the intervals recommended in your manual. The instructions should also state when and how to oil the motor to keep it operating efficiently. The condenser coils which are located outside the window may benefit from a garden-hose cleaning at the beginning of the air-conditioning season.

Cleaning Up Gas-Range Problems

When the gas range starts acting up, most people instinctively reach for the phone to call their serviceman. Actually, you can prevent or solve a number of gas-range problems, and avoid most of these costly service calls.

Here are some malfunctions you can probably take care of yourself. If these remedies don't work, *then* call a repairman.

If Nothing Happens When You Turn On the Gas for One of the Top Burners

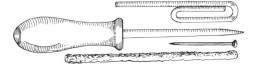

It usually means that spillovers have clogged the burner, the ignition part or the pilot part. Or a film of grease from cooking vapors can collect on air-shutter surfaces and trap dust and lint particles, which can eventually block the air-shutter opening (on the burner) and cause yellow flames and poor ignition. To prevent this, clean burners frequently as described in our section on preventive maintenance for appliances. But if tiny holes of the burners do become clogged, open them with a straight pin, paper clip, ice pick or pipe cleaner (don't use a toothpick as it could break off and cause further clogging).

If Oven Does Not Heat

Make sure the automatic oven system is off or reset for manual use, and not still in a "keep-warm" or "delayed-start" position. Be sure oven pilot is lighted (refer to instruction booklet before relighting).

If Oven Burner Is Slow to Light

A slight delay is normal—lighting can take 30 to 90 seconds, depending on the type of ignition system.

If Oven Burner Cycles Off and On

This is normal, too—it's to maintain accurately the temperatures you've selected.

If Oven Temperature Seems Too High or Too Low

Check it with a good mercury-type oven thermometer. Place thermometer in oven; turn on oven to 400F; allow to heat about 15 to 20 minutes; check temperature of oven thermometer. If after several tests, using two other temperatures, the temperature is consistently off by more than 25 degrees, it's time to call a serviceman for recalibration. In the meantime, you can adjust your oven-control dial accordingly.

If Oven Light Won't Come On

Wait until oven and light bulb are cool, and remove any covering shield. Always handle bulb with dry cloth to protect hands. The bulb may just be loose and need to be tightened. If not, replace it with a 40-watt heat-resistant oven bulb, not an ordinary light bulb. If bulb breaks during cleaning or replacing, disconnect the range's electric power at main fuse or circuit-breaker panel, or unplug range from outlet; carefully remove lamp; if the base remains in the receptacle, use pliers to grasp lamp base and remove.

If Flames Don't Issue From All Burner Ports

The ports may be blocked; clean as directed above (this applies to oven and broiler burners as well as top burners).

If Top Burner Fails To Light

Pilot is out; relight. Or the top burner may not be properly repositioned after cleaning.

If Flame Is Uneven

Ports may be clogged or burners warped. Clogs can of course be cleaned, but warped burners must be replaced.

Solving Dishwasher Problems

Modern dishwashers seem almost too good to be true. But sometimes even a dream machine malfunctions. Your dishwasher no longer sloshes with its old gusto, your dishes come out looking spotted instead of sparkling. Wait, though, before you call the serviceman. There are a number of maladies that you can handle yourself. Here are some problems and their solutions.

Spots and Film on "Clean" Dishes and Glasses

First, be sure your detergent is formulated for dishwashers—the wrong type may foam up, hampering the action. Don't add detergent until just before you're ready to start the machine; don't overfill detergent cups; don't put detergent in a wet cup. Buy detergent in small amounts (about a month's supply at a time) and store it, tightly sealed, in a dry place.

Check the water temperature—it should be 140 to 160F to be doing its job. Take a glassful of your hottest tap water and test it with a candy or meat thermometer. Then, if necessary, set your water-heater thermostat higher (remember, some heat is lost in the pipes).

Low water pressure may cause the machine to fill or rinse inadequately, so try to wash dishes when water isn't running elsewhere.

Keep an eye on drains and screens inside the dishwasher to make sure they're open, and clear any blocked jets in the spray arms.

Mineral deposits from hard water cause spotting and filming. For permanent protection, install a tank-type water softener. Otherwise, put one or two tablespoons of nonprecipitating water conditioner in the bottom of the dishwasher when detergent is added, or use an extra tablespoonful or two of detergent. A rinse aid also helps eliminate spotting.

Rinse dishes that won't be washed for an hour or so with cool water before loading the machine, or run them through a rinse-and-hold cycle if your machine has one. Other cleaning tips: Load dishes so that water can get at them—don't nest cups one inside the other. Invert cups and bowls. Alternate large and small plates. And be sure that nothing blocks the movement of the spray arms.

Wet Dishes

If your machine isn't drying dishes completely, make sure that the water is hot enough (cooler water may not evaporate entirely); dishes are loaded properly so that rinse water drains off; and the dishwasher heating element is functioning. (If this turns out to be the problem, though, only a serviceman can help.)

Discoloration of Aluminum

Though aluminum can be washed in the dishwasher, it may be darkened by the combination of detergent action and chemicals in the water. Don't place aluminum in the machine where detergent will come directly in contact with it. Hand washing is recommended for decorated or brightly colored aluminum.

Other Things to Beware of

Plastic dishes may lose their shape in high temperatures—unless the plastic is dishwasher-safe; hot water and detergent action may cause patterns on very old or hand-painted china to fade; wooden ware should be washed by hand, unless you know it's specifically okayed for dishwasher use; and cast-iron utensils should be hand washed.

Mechanical Problems

Mechanical problems are another matter, but even there you don't always have to stand by helplessly. If the motor won't run, the mechanism may be thwarted for a number of reasons: The spray arm or arms may not be revolving because a loose utensil may be protruding through the rack. If water remains a puddle beneath your dishes, the outlet in the bottom of the machine may be clogged; if so, clear it out. If the problem is that water goes everywhere—including out onto the floor—check the door to make sure it closes snugly. Or if your machine is a portable model, see if you need to straighten out crimped hoses. Other overflows may be caused by overdoses of detergent or by having the machine on a surface that is not level. Also, a simple leak in the tub sometimes may be repaired by epoxy cement. If your machine's making an awful noise, check to see if there's loose cutlery or dishes that have been loaded haphazardly and are now thrashing about inside, or if there are loose panels trembling and twitching in the machine itself.

If your problems dwarf those we've mentioned, there's only one instrument left to use—your telephone; use it to dial your local serviceman and ask for help.

If Your Freezer Stops, Keep Cool

Just because your freezer has whirred to an ominous stop, it doesn't necessarily mean you have a household crisis. As catastrophic as this may appear, don't panic! There are remedies, and in most cases your food can be saved.

Consult your instruction booklet to find out what you can do to put the freezer back in operation. Freezer conk-out may be caused by many things: a power failure in your area; a mechanical difficulty within the appliance; or even a plug that's been inadvertently disconnected. After checking the plug, call your utility company to see if they have power problems, and if so, ask how long the current will be off. If it's only for a short time, there is no problem—food will stay frozen for two days in a fully loaded freezer, and for a day or less in a freezer that's only half filled. (During the seasons when power failures are common in your community, it's a good idea to run the freezer between 10° and 20° below zero.)

If there is no power failure, there are several steps you can take before calling a serviceman or while awaiting his arrival. First, keep the door closed—open it only if you decide to retrieve the food inside. If the freezer was securely plugged in, disconnect the cord, and look for loose wires or worn insulation which might have caused a short circuit. Plug another appliance into the same outlet to see whether the fuse is at fault. Make sure the freezer-control knob is at the coldest recommended setting.

If nothing gets your freezer going, and it will take longer than a day for power to be restored or for the serviceman to arrive, you can do several things to avoid disaster. First, maybe you can find a neighbor with room enough in his or her freezer to help you out temporarily. If this doesn't work, find out if there is a freezer-locker plant in your area with space for your food, or if there's a dairy that sells dry ice (actually, you might have this information on hand well in advance of any emergency). Many freezer-locker plants offer short-term storage service for just this sort of bad moment. If you transfer to the plant, work quickly, wrapping the food in plenty of newspapers and blankets.

If you resort to dry ice, remember that a 25-pound piece will keep a half-filled 10-cubic-foot freezer at temperatures below zero for 2 or 3 days. Place the dry ice on pieces of cardboard in the freezer, not directly on top of the food. Wear gloves when handling dry ice to prevent burns. Add extra insulation by covering the freezer with blankets or quilts, being sure to leave the air vents uncovered.

Hopefully, your freezer will be restored to health before food damage occurs. But keep in mind that any food has a better chance of survival if care has been taken in the preparation, packaging, and freezing of it. The more sanitary you are in readying food for the freezer, the better it will withstand a freezer "blackout"—sanitary preparation means fewer bacteria to cause spoilage. Frozen bacteria are not dead, however, and when they warm up they become active. So, if you find that despite your efforts, the food has started to thaw, then you have three choices: refreeze some of the food; cook the food, and then refreeze it; or throw it away.

When the freezer's ailment has been properly diagnosed and it is ready to receive frozen foods again, be sure to clean the inside thoroughly and allow it to dry before refilling.

To Refreeze Thawed Food

The most important factor to consider when refreezing food is how cold it still is. A thermometer in the freezer gives you the answer. Food bacteria will not grow in foods that are below 38°F, and grow slowly as long as the temperatures remain under 45°.

Foods that are still cold—about 40°—or that still have some ice crystals are usually good candidates for refreezing. Squeeze the package to feel whether the food is still firm, with crystals in the center. If the food has changed in color or odor, these are sure signs of spoilage—throw it out.

What refreezes well? Meats and poultry with no signs of spoilage. Fruits, too. But vegetables, shellfish, and packaged precooked foods that have started to thaw and cannot be used immediately should be discarded, since it's difficult to tell whether they are still good.

If you are going to refreeze thawed food, it might be wise to take it to a commercial freezer-locker plant for really fast freezing. If this is not possible, turn the freezer's adjustable control to the coldest position until the food is well frozen. Then adjust the freezer control to its usual setting.

To Cook Thawed Foods for Refreezing

Food that is completely thawed can be saved, too—if it is cooked, then refrozen. Thawed chicken, for instance, can be cooked, the meat removed from the bones, and the results frozen in separately wrapped packages for future use in casseroles and dishes like chicken à la king. Thawed ground beef can be made into meatballs that can be cooked and frozen for spaghetti suppers later. Ground beef can also be browned, thoroughly cooked, and frozen for quick use later. Or it can be made into a baked meat loaf which would be delicious for sandwiches at another time. Thawed fruits, like strawberries, are perfect for jams, jellies, and pie fillings. There are many ways to cook and refreeze thawed foods, so check your favorite cookbook.

Curing
Your Sick
Vacuum Cleaner

If your vacuum cleaner has lost its spunk and pickup, the fault is seldom in the mechanism. Rather, it is most often a simple matter of improper use and maintenance. Sometimes a part needs replacing. You can easily do these repairs yourself. First, read your instruction book thoroughly. Refer to it frequently. Its detailed illustrations are very helpful. Here are some other tips for coping with the most common ailments.

Vacuum Cleaner Doesn't Pick Up Dirt

The bag is probably too full. A cleaner is at peak efficiency, with best suction power, when the bag is empty; as the bag fills, efficiency decreases. The frequency with which you change the bag will depend greatly on the type of dirt you're picking up. For example, fluff from a new sheared carpet may fill the bag, yet cleaning efficiency will remain reasonably high. Fluff is light and porous, and does not restrict airflow through the bag. The reverse occurs when fine dirt and dust are picked up. Vacuuming a concrete floor, workshop, or garage can quickly impede airflow. Even with a bag that appears to be only half full, a film of fine dust can clog the bag's pores. Check frequently.

While fluff may not restrict the airflow, you should not allow the bag to overfill. Some fluff may back up into cleaner parts and block the airflow in the hose of a canister, in the exhaust area, or in the dirt channel of an upright cleaner. The fluff from new, sheared carpets may persist through many vacuumings, and clogging might inadvertently occur in these parts. Check and clear any accumulation each time the bag is changed. It is important to replace the bag with one specified by the manufacturer of your cleaner.

If the bag is new and the cleaner still doesn't pick up dirt, the filter may need cleaning. For a cleaner to develop airflow and suction, the porous paper filter or the permanent plastic filter must be clean. The permanent plastic filter covering the motor should be removed periodically and washed in warm, sudsy water, rinsed thoroughly, and gently dried. To avoid motor damage, be sure the filter is thoroughly dry when it is reattached. Paper filters should be replaced.

When the hose and wands of a canister cleaner become clogged, check them for large objects—children's blocks, toy cars, etc. Disconnect the hose from the cleaner, and turn the power on. Place your hand over the hose opening on the cleaner. If the cleaner is still producing suction power with the hose detached, then something is blocking the hose or wands. Take a broom or mop handle, and gently push it through the hose or wand. The object should fall out. Hoses may also be cleared by attaching them to the blower opening on the cleaner and blowing hose clean. (Do it outdoors!)

The rubber drive belt or belts on upright cleaners may stretch, wear, or break after long usage. They can easily be replaced at home. Your instruction book will tell you how to do it. Replace the old belt with one specifically made for your model cleaner. (This can be purchased at hardware stores, vacuum-cleaner shops, or by writing to the manufacturer.) If the belt breaks frequently, the agitator or brush-roll bearings should be lubricated by a service center.

If your cleaner has a suction-adjustment control, make sure it is correctly set for the particular carpet being cleaned. Very thin or loosely woven carpeting requires a low suction position; indoor/outdoor, sculptured, or multilevel rugs require a high setting for most effective and proper cleaning.

Shag rugs, which are very popular today, may present special problems. Some cleaners adjust automatically, or have a shag setting or a special tool attachment for these. Cleaning strokes should be short, overlapping, and repetitive to allow the cleaner suction and brush action to deep-clean the carpet effectively.

If the brush bristles are worn, they won't make proper contact with the carpet surface and won't pick up lint and small particles. The brush should be adjusted periodically to a lower setting if your vacuum has this feature; otherwise, the brushes should be replaced. An easy test for worn brushes: Hold the edge of a card across the nozzle; if bristles don't touch the card, they should be replaced or adjusted. Your cleaner does not pick up better by pressing down hard on the nozzle. Efficient cleaning depends on the number of strokes combined with the suction. All you'll get from pressing down is a sore back!

The Bag Breaks

This is usually caused by very fine particles, such as ash, cement dust, plaster dust, or powder, filling the pores of the paper bag and preventing air from passing through. Pressure builds up until the bag breaks. Replace bag frequently when picking up such materials. Don't use a vacuum cleaner to remove fireplace or furnace ashes. If your cleaner has a soft outer bag, avoid bumping it into sharp corners.

Cleaner is Noisy

Check fan for any solid object lodged in it. Agitator bearings or motor bearings may need lubrication, but this must be done by a service center.

Your vacuum cleaner will serve you best if you keep it clean inside and out. Remove lint and hair from attachment brushes with an old comb, and wash periodically in mild, sudsy water, rinsing and drying thoroughly. After cleaning a particularly messy area, tools should be cleaned immediately. The interior shell of a canister and dust-bag cover of upright cleaner should be cleaned periodically with a damp cloth. Hair, string, or threads on the brush or agitator should be removed often.

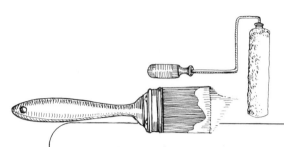

What to Do When Your Old Paint Job Fades Away

As your survey a room in your house that needs painting, do you feel the walls closing in? If you haven't quite summoned up the confidence to tackle the problem, it's time you knew that today's paint and equipment are easier than ever to use. And by wielding a brush yourself, the cost will be much less than you might expect.

Paint Selection

There are two basic types of paint—latex, which is water soluble; and oil-based, which is solvent-soluble. Latex is probably the most popular because it is easy to apply, fast drying, and brushes and rollers are easily cleaned in soap and water. Oil-based paints are very durable, highly resistant to staining and damage, and can take frequent scrubbings—but they also take longer to dry. Both types are available in gloss, semigloss and flat finishes.

Painting is most successful with good-quality paint—it covers better (in most cases only one coat will be needed), lasts longer, spatters less, is less likely to peel, is easy to work with, gives a smoother finish and is less likely to show brush marks. Though paint can be purchased for as little as $2 a gallon, high-quality paint can run to $8 or $9 a gallon—but in terms of time and energy saved, it's worth the higher price.

How much paint will you need? Determine the square feet of each surface you want to cover (multiply the length of the area by its width—and don't bother to subtract for window and door openings unless they are especially large); then add all square feet together to get the total area you'll be working on. The label on each gallon paint can tells you how far the contents will go (usually it's 400 to 500 square feet) so you can easily calculate how many cans you'll need to do the job.

Surface Preparation

Remove pictures, wall accessories, lamps and small pieces of furniture; move large furniture to center of room and cover with newspapers, large pieces of plastic, old blankets or sheets or drop cloths. Roll up and remove rug if possible. Cover floor with papers. Remove light-switch plates and any other fixtures that come off. Wipe ceilings, walls and woodwork with clean, dry cloth; or vacuum to remove dust. In kitchens and bathrooms, wash walls and ceilings to remove grease and dirt. If there are cracks or holes in the surface to be painted, fill tiny fissures with a ready-to-use plaster pencil; for more gaping problems, use a ready-mixed spackling compound—it should fill the breach quickly and easily.

Rollers and Brushes

Here again, good-quality rollers and brushes are a must. Rollers are simple to use and are the most popular way to paint large areas such as walls and ceilings (you'll still need a brush, though, for trim and edging). When purchasing a roller, keep in mind the surface you'll be working on—the rougher it is, the deeper the nap of the roller cover will have to be in order to squish into depressions and cracks. Synthetic roller covers such as nylon, modacrylic and polyurethane foam are best suited for latex paint, though they're perfectly satisfactory for oil-based paints, too. Lamb's wool and rayon covers are good for oil-based paints, but *not* for latex paints because water will soften the fibers and cause them to swell.

Good brushes have long bristles that are tapered and flagged (or split) at the ends, have a springy feel and don't break or fall out. Bristles are of two types: Synthetic ones of nylon or polyester are best for latex but may be used for any paint; natural bristles should be used only for oil paints.

Painting Techniques

Start with the ceiling. Paint across the width of the room in strips about two feet wide. Start each new strip before the previous one has dried, and overlap the strips as you go. For walls, brush-paint a border next to all trim and in corners—then, when rolling or brushing begins in earnest, you won't have to worry about splattering edges.

When using a brush, stroke the paint on with moderate pressure, smoothing the effect by lifting brush lightly at the end of each stroke. When using a roller, it seems easier to get the paint on the working surface first and then to spread it evenly. To do this, paint a large inverted V or W on the particular area you're working on, making your first stroke from bottom to top. Then move roller back and forth to spread and smooth out paint.

Post-Painting Wrap-Up

Brushes and rollers should be cleaned immediately after use. Latex paint comes out with soap and water. Oil-based paint needs more coaxing: Soak rollers or brushes in turpentine or thinner until paint loosens; work bristles or roller covers against bottom of the container in which you're soaking; then rinse again in fresh turpentine until all is clear. Comb bristles smooth. When rollers and brushes are dry, wrap them in heavy paper or foil and hang up or store flat.

How To Wipe Out Wallpaper Woes

Have you thought about papering a room but decided it was a job for professionals? Then it's time you knew that nobody has to be a wallflower about wallpapering. It has been simplified by prepasted wall coverings, but no matter what type wall covering, follow these steps to complete the project.

Tools

For most papering jobs you'll need a broad, flexible brush to apply paste; razor-sharp cutter and paper shears; smoothing brush; chalk line and plumb bob (make your own with a weighted chalk-coated string); seam roller; yardstick; stepladder; bowl of water and sponge; paste and bucket (or a water pan if you're using prepasted paper). You may also need sizing, patching plaster, sandpaper and wall scraper, and a large surface to prepare the paper for hanging will definitely be needed.

Wall Covering Required

Measure height of wall in feet from ceiling to baseboard; measure distance around the room at the baseboard. Multiply height by width of each door, window or other area *not* to be covered.

Multiply height by width of each wall surface, subtract the square footage of the doors and windows. Figure that each roll of paper gives you 30 square feet of coverage (there are actually 36 square feet in a roll). Divide total area by 30 to get number of rolls needed.

Preparation

If the walls were painted with a gloss or semi-gloss paint, sand with a medium-grade sandpaper. Wash with an all-purpose cleaning solution; rinse and let dry; apply sizing; dry. For plaster walls, scrape off peeling paint and plaster; firm up loose plaster with a patching compound; smooth; let dry; sand with medium sandpaper. Cover newly plastered walls with flat primer sealer. For dry walls, tape and spackle joints and seams. Hammer in protruding nails; cover dent with spackle, level; dry; apply second coat; dry. For walls already papered, vinyl-coated wall coverings should be removed. Remove strippable and fabric-backed vinyl wall coverings by loosening a corner and peeling. If there are more than two layers of wallpaper, remove the old paper; an electric steamer can be rented to help. When wall covering is removed, wash off scraps of paper or glue with steel wool and wallpaper-remover solution. Wash walls with all-purpose cleaning solution and steel wool; rinse with clean water; dry; apply sizing.

Measuring and Hanging

Measure width of the paper and subtract one inch (the inch fits around door casing—a good place to begin—and is trimmed away later). From the right edge of the door, measure out the above width and make a pencil mark. Tack plumb line near the ceiling directly above the point where mark was made. Pull weight at end of plumb line tight and pluck the string—it leaves a vertical chalk mark on the wall. Measure the wall height. Unroll paper with pattern side up. Cut first strip six inches longer than wall height (for trim at top and bottom). Lay second strip next to first strip to match pattern; cut same length as the first.

Read directions before mixing paste. Turn wallpaper strip face down on the table; apply paste to bottom section; fold paper toward center without creasing; do same to opposite section; get edges even as you fold. Wait three to five minutes. Unfold top section and place on the wall so it overlaps the ceiling joint about two inches. Line up one edge with the plumb line. Smooth down upper section with smoothing brush. Open lower folded section and slide into position. Check for alignment with plumb line, then brush. Using a wall scraper as a guide, trim excess material with a razor-blade cutter. Before paste dries (after each strip is applied), rinse baseboards, casings and ceiling moldings. Wipe the newly hung strip with damp sponge. Hang the next strip the same way, using the edge of first strip as a vertical guide; don't overlap. After 15 minutes, roll seams with a roller. Each time you begin a new wall, drop a plumb line.

When using prepasted wall coverings, read directions carefully. Reroll the strips from bottom to top with pattern inside—roll loosely so the water reaches the entire prepasted surface. Place water pan at baseboard and hang in same manner as other wall coverings.

Repairing Plaster-Wall Damage

Besides being unsightly, wall cracks and holes can be havens for insects and moisture. With a few simple tools and supplies, however, you can easily repair the damage.

There are three types of patching compound: ready-mix spackling, which is easy to use and is good for small jobs; powdered spackling, which is mixed with water and is cheaper, practical for major repairs, but sets more slowly; and patching plaster, also mixed with water, which is the least expensive and is used to patch large holes and cracks. You'll need a putty knife at least three inches wide, a screwdriver or other sharp tool, medium-grit sandpaper and a stiff brush.

Begin the repair by removing loose plaster in and around the hole or crack; use a beer-can opener, or other sharp pointed tool. Then undercut the edges of the crack, making the inside of the crack wider than the outside, to provide a good anchor for the patching compound when pressed into place. Clean out dust and loose material with a stiff brush. Dampen the surface of the crack to prevent the old plaster from absorbing moisture from the new.

Prepare patching compound according to directions on the package. If using patching powder, mix only a small amount at a time; it hardens quickly, so do not mix until ready to use. Scoop up patching compound with putty knife and press the mixture in until it completely fills the hole. Smooth outer surface, holding the putty knife so the blade is almost flat against the wall, and crisscross the surface several times to remove excess compound. Let the patch dry at least 24 hours; if the filling shrinks at all, dampen again and fill in any hollow spots with a second coat. When dry, smooth by using sandpaper wrapped around a small piece of wood. If painting is to follow, use a primer-sealer over the patch to prevent the repaired spot from absorbing more paint than the surrounding area. (The primer-sealer can be eliminated if you're using latex paints.)

Several layers of patching compound will be required for cracks over a quarter inch wide or holes much larger than the size of a nail. First, fill the crack or hole only halfway, and allow to dry until hard; then fill even with the surface. Depending on the size of the hole, a third application may be necessary. When hard, smooth with sandpaper.

If you need to repair a large section of plaster that has buckled, or a deep crack that protrudes through to the supporting strip of wood underneath, a bit more work is involved. Prepare the area by chipping out all the damaged plaster with a chisel and hammer (a putty knife may work). Undercut solid material remaining around the edges. Rather than applying one thick coat of plaster, which could shrink and even crack as it dries, build the patch in layers. In addition to a putty knife, a square trowel is handy for spreading the layers of plaster evenly. Thoroughly wet the area to be patched with water and a brush. Apply first coat of plaster with putty knife, packing firmly around edges; fill about halfway. Leave this first coat rough to provide a good bond for the next. When dry, wet again, and apply second coat with trowel, making the patch level with the outer surface. Apply enough pressure with the trowel to pack the plaster tightly. Smooth surface with trowel, let dry and sand.

If there is a large hole without backing, fill in first with wadded newspaper to provide a backing for the plaster. If you have any trouble getting the plaster to adhere to the paper, cover paper with wire mesh. Patch by working in from the edge toward the center; let dry. Apply another layer around the new edge, repeating the applications until the hole is completely filled. Sand until smooth.

If wall has a textured surface, make the patch match it while plaster is still wet, using a sponge or comb.

If crevices and deep pits cover most of a wall, if large areas of cracks form on the ceiling or if cracks form in the walls of a new house settling into its foundation, don't tackle the job yourself. This is the time to call in a professional plasterer.

New Life For Old Rooms with Wall Paneling

Professional-looking paneled walls can be easily achieved by the do-it-yourselfer. The directions here are for nailing panels to furred-out walls (furring means adding wood strips to existing walls). This is necessary because some walls are uneven and because furring provides a smooth surface on which to apply the paneling. Most furring strips are one inch by two inches—about 120 feet are needed for an eight-by-12-foot wall. Other equipment includes a hand or electric saw, hammer, level, plumb line, small compass, nails ($2\frac{1}{2}$-inch regular nails and $1\frac{5}{8}$-inch finishing nails). Finishing nails may be eliminated if you use a tool called a nail gun; it looks like a staple gun but countersinks wood-tone nails (to match paneling) without marring the panel's surface. If finishing nails are used, holes may be filled with a putty stick in the same color as paneling.

Prefinished panels vary greatly in price, from under $10 to $50 or more for the usual four-by-eight-foot panel (nine- or 12-foot ones may be custom ordered). When ordering from your lumber dealer or home-improvement center, make a rough sketch of the room that shows window, door and other openings, plus complete dimensions of the room. The dealer can then give you the exact number of panels that you will need.

Store panels flat in the room in which they will be used for about two days so that they can adjust to the humidity; separate them so air gets to faces and backs. In the meantime, pry off all ceiling and floor moldings, which will be replaced later with panel-matched molding. Find studs in the wall and mark the locations. If you locate the nail holes where the floor molding or baseboard was fastened, the studs should line up vertically with the holes. Or you can buy a magnetic stud finder at the hardware store. Once the first stud is located, the others will be easy to find as they're spaced 16 inches apart, measuring from center to center.

Now you're ready to put up furring strips. With 2½-inch nails, place a furring strip vertically in the corner of each wall, then over studs at 48-inch intervals. Fasten a strip, horizontally, at top and bottom of each wall and continue to fill the wall with strips at 16-inch intervals. Stand panels around the room against the walls, positioning them for the most pleasing effect in color and grain. Number them on the back in sequence so they don't get mixed up.

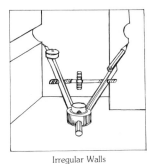

Irregular Walls

To install panels, start at a left-hand corner. If corner is straight, place the first panel against the wall, and nail into place. If wall is irregular—against a brick fireplace, for example—place the first panel two inches from left corner and line up the edge with a level or plumb line. Use a compass to mark the panel edge with the exact outline of the edge of the left-hand wall; then cut or plane the left edge of the panel along marked line. When panel is fitted in place, be sure that the right edge falls over a vertical furring strip nailed to a stud; if it doesn't, trim it down until it does. Subsequent panels should then automatically line up properly.

Nail panel into place with finishing nails spaced six inches apart at top and bottom and 12 inches apart on horizontal and vertical furring strips. To continue with the next panels, butt edges against previously installed one (tap against the right-hand edge of the panel, using a wood block between the paneling and the hammer). Make sure to maintain a true vertical line, then nail into place.

To cut around openings, measure carefully from the right edge of the previous panel to the doorway or window frame and transfer measurements to the next panel with a soft pencil and metal straightedge. Cut, fit and nail. Exact measurements for cutouts of electrical outlets, switch plates, heat registers, and so on, are important. After the panel has been properly cut for fit, rub face of opening (such as outlet box) generously with chalk. Place panel on wall and tap at outlet location; this transfers image to back of panel to indicate the area for cutting. Drill holes at corners of the cutout area; cut out the section with saber or keyhole saw.

Measure and trim the last panel as accurately as the first. To finish the walls, install prefinished moldings that harmonize with the paneling over all the seams and joints at ceilings, floors and corners. For a professional-looking job and perfect fit, be sure to miter the corner moldings.

Replacing Ceramic Wall Tiles

Ceramic tile is tough. But it can become chipped or cracked, and sometimes entire tiles will come loose. Such damage looks unsightly, but repairs are not difficult. Replacements are available at building-supply or hardware stores, and you will probably be able to match your old tiles exactly—or at least come quite close. In addition to the familiar square tiles available, you can also buy the pieces needed for trimming at top and edges. If you're replacing a large expanse of tile, or tiling a wall for the first time, you may wish to use the pregrouted glazed ceramic tile available in two-foot-square sheets—the sheets have already been grouted with silicone rubber, which makes them flexible and convenient for you to install.

To replace tiles you'll need these basic tools: chisel, hammer, sponge, adhesive, grout and a trowel or similar kind of spreader. If you need to cut a tile for a specially shaped area, you will need ceramic nippers, a cutting tool that can be bought inexpensively or even rented at a tile store.

The tile adhesive you use can either be mortar cement, which requires mixing, or the more convenient ready-mixed tile cement, or even tub-and-tile caulking that comes in a tube. Grout is the material used to fill the spaces between tiles; it is available in powder form that must be mixed with water, but it can also be purchased at hardware and tile stores in a form that is mixed and ready to go on your walls.

Three important rules: When removing a damaged tile, wear glasses or goggles to protect your eyes from any sharp flying chips; wear rubber or plastic gloves to protect your hands from caustic materials; clean and smooth the surface where the new tile is to go (remove all lumpy traces of old adhesive), so it will fit flush and firmly with surrounding tile.

The damaged tile must first be removed, and you must take care not to damage surrounding tiles while doing so. Remove as much of the grout as possible from around the tile by scraping out the material with a sharp-pointed instrument (the corner of a stiff putty knife or a chisel or can opener should do). Next, tap at all four corners of the tile with a chisel and hammer, chipping a little at a time while working your way toward center of tile. Then remove the center itself by prying with the chisel and by tapping lightly with a hammer if extra force is necessary.

When the damaged tile has been removed, carefully clean the opening, removing any remaining cement and making the undersurface completely smooth. If you are replacing a loose tile, scrape any adhesive from its back so it is clean. Before cementing down the new tile, place it in the cavity, and if it doesn't fit, sand the edges until it does. Most tiles have built-in spacing lugs—little humps at their edges to provide grout space. If it's necessary to sand these off to make the tile fit, you can allow for grout spacing by sticking toothpicks in at the bottom of the new tile.

To cement the new tile in place, apply just enough adhesive so that it will not ooze out when tile is fitted into place. Then press tile firmly into position on the wall, making sure it lines up with surrounding tiles and is accurately centered. Allow the tile to dry for 12 to 24 hours. If spacing lugs were sanded away and you're using toothpicks, leave them there during the drying period to prevent the tile from slipping out of position; remove them when you're ready for grout.

After drying is complete, apply grouting material into open spaces around the newly installed tile. Use a sponge or cloth to wipe the grout into the spaces, then run a rounded implement, such as the end of an old toothbrush, over the grout to make a smooth surface. Allow it to dry overnight, wash off any of the excess grout with a wet sponge, and buff dry with a towel to bring out the shine of the glazed surface.

Bringing Old Floors Back to Life

Nothing is more beautiful than the rich glow of a natural wood floor, but it takes work. And even with frequent waxing and polishing, the day will come when your floor becomes so scuffed and dingy that refinishing is the only solution.

Previous finishes must be completely removed and the floor must be bare, smooth, clean, free of dust and wax, and dry before a new finish is applied. Liquid paint and varnish removers are sometimes used to strip small areas—such as a closet floor or rug border—or when finish or paint is difficult to remove. But for removing old finishes from an entire wood floor, power sanding is the most practical and effective method.

A complete sanding job requires special equipment: a drum sander; a disc-edge sander; a hand scraper; and abrasive paper in various grades. Electric sanders can be rented for a nominal fee at large hardware, paint and "U-rent-it" stores—and an ample supply of abrasive papers will come with the machine as well as directions for use. Rather than push the sander, hold on and let it move slowly across the floor by its own power. The disc-edge sander can then finish the job—it moves in along baseboards and other inaccessible areas. The hand scraper is used in corners or other crannies.

Before sanding begins, remove everything from the room; open all windows and close doors to adjoining rooms.

A major sanding job is done in three steps, with three grades of paper. The purpose of the *first sanding* is to remove the old finish down to the bare wood. Coarse, open-coat No. 3½ or 20-grit sandpaper is called for. Pass the drum sander slowly over the floor lengthwise, going with the grain of the wood. Start at one wall and move straight along the grain to the opposite wall, then walk backwards, pulling the sander back along the same path. As you move again from wall to wall, overlap each previous pass by about two or three inches and return, completing the floor in this fashion. Use edger with the same grade of sandpaper to sand close to walls; use the hand scraper for even more difficult spots.

Change to a medium, No. ½ or 40-grit sandpaper. Pass the sander over the floor, using the same technique as before. Put the same medium paper on the edge sander to finish borders. There is one more step—*final sanding*. Use a fine No. 2/0 or 100-grit sandpaper, and sand as before. Now vacuum or sweep to clean up all the dust.

Whether or not you stain the floor before applying the finish is a matter of personal choice. Consult the label of the finishing material you plan to use to be sure the product can be applied over stain.

The final part of the refinishing job is the application of the floor finish. Finishes generally fall into two categories: surface finishes and penetrating floor sealers.

Surface finishes: *Shellac* is economical, flexible and quick-drying. Properly applied, it wears well. It is easily patched; if a spot becomes worn, it can be sanded and cleaned and a new application of shellac feathered in so it is barely noticeable. Shellac is of two types—orange and white. White shellac darkens the wood less than orange. Because shellac has a low resistance to water and other liquids, it must be waxed for protection.

Varnish is available in a wide range of qualities and prices.

Poor quality, cheap varnishes tend to become brittle or show white scars. Varnish is slow-drying, and though there are some "quick-dry" varnishes, they are often less durable than regular ones. Abrasion resistance is high, particularly with a urethane formula. Varnish is more water-resistant than shellac, but it is susceptible to scratching and becomes darker with age.

Penetrating finishes: These floor finishes put tough resins *in* the wood rather than *on* it. The resins harden the wood, making it very wear-resistant. Like shellac, penetrating finishes can be touched up easily, and they are the easiest of all to apply—just brush the finish on, allow it to sink in, then wipe.

After sufficient drying time, apply a thin coat of paste or liquid polishing wax; buff with an electric floor polisher.

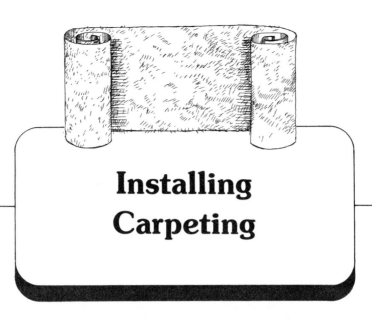

Installing
Carpeting

Wall-to-wall carpeting can add comfort and warmth to any room, and you don't have to ruin your budget having it installed. Doing it yourself is not all that difficult. Carpet installation kits that contain basic cutting and carpet-laying tools are inexpensive and available in the floor-covering sections of department stores, hardware stores and from carpet companies. Other tools you might need, such as a knee kicker (a tool to stretch carpet flat) and staple gun, can be rented.

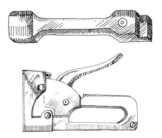

Consider laying padding under the carpeting as it extends carpet life, adds comfort and insulates against heat, cold and noise. Carpet with foam-rubber backing eliminates the need for a separate pad.

Preparing a Room for Carpeting

First, remove all furniture from the room and clean the floor thoroughly; it must be free of dirt and wax. Carpeting may be installed on just about any surface—wood, resilient tile or cement. If the floor has loose or warped boards, they should be nailed down; missing or loose tiles should be replaced or tacked down. Concrete floors should be vacuumed, washed and allowed to dry thoroughly. Carefully remove molding at floor level. Check all door clearances into the room; use a scrap of carpeting (plus padding if you intend to install it) to see if the door can open and close over it. If there isn't sufficient clearance, the bottom of the door must be trimmed.

There are various methods of adhering carpet to the floor. "Tackless" fastening involves the use of plywood strips containing tacks which are placed around the perimeter of the room. The carpet is then stretched onto the tacks. This method is usually used with jute-backed or woven carpeting. Other methods include double-face tape or adhesives. (Tape and adhesives work best at room temperature. Don't attempt the job if the floor temperature is below 55 degrees.) On concrete or brick floors a tackless strip is fastened to the floor with adhesive or secured with masonry nails.

To Lay Foam-Backed Carpeting

Apply double-face carpeting tape around the perimeter of the room (don't peel off protective paper at this point). Cut the carpet to size, allowing three to four inches excess to run up each wall. Position carpet on the floor. Using a carpet-protective cutting board (a specially designed board that comes as part of a kit or is available at hardware stores), push the carpet snugly into room corners. At the same time, slit the carpet down each corner with a utility knife; this allows the carpet to lie flat. Fold back the carpet, one corner at a time, and peel off the paper from the tape. Then press the carpet back into position by smoothing from the center of the room toward the corner and press the carpet onto tape.

Trim the corners first by pushing the protective cutting board into each corner to compress the carpet; cut from corner about five inches in each direction. Use the board to force the carpet snugly between wall and floor. Then trim excess carpet.

To Lay Carpet Without Foam Backing

Here directions will include the use of "tackless" strips and padding. The strips are nailed to the floor, with the tacks facing toward the walls, around the entire perimeter of the room (they may be cut with a pair of tin snips). Then put the carpet pad down. It should be cut to fit inside the rim of the strips, not on top of them. Adhere the pad to the floor with a staple gun. Lay out the carpet, and cut flush with the wall. A knee kicker is used to stretch carpet flat; the dial on it is adjustable so its teeth won't dig into the carpet backing (long-pile carpets require a higher number, short-pile a lower number). Hold the tool by its neck and hit the pad of the knee kicker with your knee in order to push the carpet onto the "tackless" strip. Repeat this all along the edges until carpet is stretched tight and smooth. Then go back and trim the carpet flush with wall and tuck the edges behind the strip with a screwdriver or a similar blunt tool.

Removing Furniture Scars

When wood furniture is badly damaged, a professional finisher or cabinetmaker should be consulted. But the home handyperson can deal with most minor forms of damage.

Keep these general points in mind: (1) Furniture finishes are fragile, so proceed with caution. (2) A household or commercial remedy should be pretested in an inconspicuous spot. (3) Avoid harsh rubbing and overapplication of remedies. (4) Always rub in the direction of the grain of the wood. (5) Remember that no one remedy is a cure-all. (6) Repair products we suggest may be obtained at hardware stores, supermarkets, and, in some cases, drugstores.

Minor Scratches and Blemishes

If the blemish has not yet penetrated the finish, an application of paste, liquid, or cream wax will sometimes hide the mark. If not, gently rub the wax in with fine (3/0) steel wool, and then polish. If blemish remains, remove wax by rubbing the area with naphtha. Wipe dry with a clean cloth, and try one of the following: Rub with half a Brazil nut or black walnut (the nut oil may provide enough coloring to hide a minor scratch). Or color the blemish with brown crayon or wood-toned furniture-wax stick, then rub in well, and wipe with a soft, dry cloth. For scratches on red-finished mahogany, use new iodine; on brown or cherry mahogany, use iodine that is dark-brown with age; on maple, dilute new iodine about 50 percent with denatured alcohol. You might also try rottenstone. Buy a small amount from a paint or hardware store. Put it in an old saltshaker. Pour a few drops of salad oil on the blemish, and shake on enough rottenstone to make a paste; then rub briskly with a soft, clean cloth. Frequently compare the gloss of damaged area with original finish.

Nail-Polish Stain

Rub with 3/0 steel wool dipped in liquid or cream wax.

Paint Stains

If fresh, the stain can be removed by rubbing with 3/0 steel wool dipped in liquid or cream wax. For old paint stains, cover the area with linseed oil, and wait until paint softens. Wipe with cloth soaked in linseed oil. Remove any remaining paint with rotten-stone treatment.

Severe Burns and Blemishes

For deeper damage, follow these steps: (1) Scrape blemish clean with sharp knife or razor blade. Remove loose dirt or charred wood; clean scraped-out area with naphtha. (2) Smooth area with 3/0 steel wool wrapped around end of wooden skewer or orange stick. Clean again with naphtha. Rub with fine sandpaper or emery board. (3) Purchase $\frac{1}{4}$ pint oil stain of the proper color. (For light wood, dilute $\frac{1}{4}$ teaspoon stain with a few drops of naphtha or turpentine.) Apply with tiny brush or cotton swab, wiping with cloth and reapplying until stain matches the original finish. Let dry 12 hours. (4) Fill damaged area with stick shellac that matches the wood finish. First, heat metal-spatula blade over alcohol flame of electric unit (soot from gas or candle may discolor shellac). Blade should be just hot enough to melt shellac. Then scrape off a bit of shellac, and press into blemish with edge of the blade. Repeat until filled. (5) Heat spatula blade, wipe clean, and scrape across patch to level. Shave off excess shellac with razor blade. (6) Sand with very fine (8/0) sandpaper, or fine side of emery board, rubbing lightly with grain of wood until scratch is even with the finish. (7) Rub with rottenstone and oil, as previously directed, and polish with paste wax.

Candle Wax

Put an ice cube on the wax for a few seconds, and wipe up water immediately. With fingers, peel off as much wax as possible; then scrape gently with dull knife. Rub briskly with cloth saturated with liquid or cream wax, and dry with a clean cloth. Repeat until mark disappears.

Milk Spots

When milk, or food containing milk or cream, remains on furniture, the effect of the lactic acid is similar to that of a mild paint or varnish remover. Clean with cream wax, then follow instructions for removing alcohol spots.

Water Marks

Apply paste wax with 3/0 steel wool. Or, place clean, thick blotter over the ring, and press with warm (not hot) iron. Repeat until ring disappears. Or, try the rottenstone or camphorated-oil treatment.

Alcohol Spots

An alcohol spill should be wiped up immediately because it can quickly cause damage. If a spot remains, there are several ways to treat it. Rub with finger dipped in furniture wax, linseed oil, or moistened cigar ash. Rewax. With some finishes, a quick application of ammonia will work; put a few drops on a damp cloth, and rub the spot. Follow with rewaxing. If treatment has been delayed, mix rottenstone and a few drops of linseed oil or salad oil into a creamy paste. Apply the paste with a soft cloth, rubbing with the grain. Powdered pumice is a harder abrasive and may be substituted, if necessary. Finish with rottenstone treatment.

White Spots or Rings—cause unknown

Rub blemish with cigarette or cigar ashes, using cloth dipped in liquid or cream wax, lubricating oil, vegetable shortening, or salad oil. Wipe off immediately, and rewax. You might also try rubbing rottenstone or table salt on blemish with a cloth dipped in any of the above lubricants. Or, with a cloth, rub on a thick paste of powdered pumice and linseed oil. Use a cloth moistened with naphtha to wipe surface for inspection. Finish by rubbing with rottenstone and oil.

Yellow Spots on Light Wood

As bleached or blond furniture ages, it tends to darken because the chemicals used to bleach out the natural wood lose their effectiveness. But the discoloring is gradual and hardly noticeable unless the older wood is compared with a new piece of furniture. When exposed to direct sunlight, light woods may darken in just a few days and unsightly yellow spots may appear. Unfortunately, there is no remedy for removing these yellow spots or for the change of color.

Ink Stains

Difficult to remove. On a waxed finish, an ink spill, if blotted immediately, may not leave a spot. But if the mark has penetrated, try the rottenstone treatment.

Heat Marks

These white blemishes are usually quite difficult to remove without complete refinishing. But the following treatment may work: Stroke area lightly with nonlinty cloth moistened with camphorated oil. Wipe immediately with clean cloth. If rough, rub with 3/0 steel wool dipped in paste wax or lubricating oil. Rottenstone treatment might also be tried.

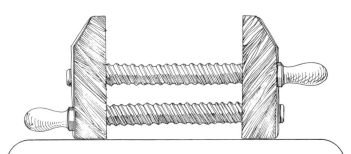

Healing Your Sick Furniture

Wobbly chair or table? Sticking drawer? Loose veneer? If these are problems around your home, a good wood glue, a few specialized tools, and some handyperson know-how can remedy them.

Wobbly Chair or Table

Wobbliness is usually caused by a loose rung in the legs, or a frame that has loosened around the bottom of the chair seat or tabletop.

To reglue a chair rung: It's easily accomplished if you can remove the rung. But don't remove the rung unless you can do so without damaging the piece. Scrape off old glue from end of rung and around rung hole. (Scrape the hole carefully so it doesn't become enlarged.) Apply wood glue generously to end of rung and also into the hole and reassemble by forcing rung back into place. Wipe off excess glue. Another way to tighten loose joints is to coat fine silk thread with glue and wrap it around end of the rung; then apply more glue to the thread, and push rung back into its hole.

If joints are so snug that the rung cannot be removed completely, drill a hole into the joint from the outside of leg, penetrating only as far as the rung. Force glue into the joint through the hole. There is a special glue injector sold for this purpose. Or you can use an oiler, a gadget that works like a hypodermic needle but is filled with glue rather than oil. Use a wood putty of matching color to cover the hole in the chair leg.

After regluing, pressure should be applied with any of several tools: cabinetmaker's clamps, long bar clamps; bell-type webbing clamps, or a plain rope tourniquet (see figure A). Tie the rope loosely around the outside of the legs, placing wads of paper as cushioning where the rope touches the legs. Use a small stick to twist the rope tightly (tourniquet fashion), and tie after sufficient pressure has been applied.

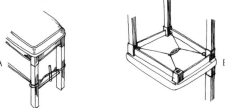

A   B

To repair loose joints at frame area of chairs and tables, install corner braces on the underside. Cut triangular wood blocks to fit the four corners; then glue and screw into each corner. If there are braces already in place, fresh glue and larger screws will strengthen them.

Problems with creaky chair frames can also be solved with heavy picture wire and screw eyes (see figure B). Screw one eye into the top of the leg in each corner. Cut two pieces of picture wire. Fasten the end of one to an eye, thread it through a turnbuckle (purchased from a hardware store), and fasten it to the eye on the same side of the frame. Repeat with second strand on the opposite side. Glue the corner joints of the chair, and then use turnbuckle to draw the wires into a tight position. It also serves as a brace for the framework.

Sticking Drawers

In damp weather, drawers stick because of temporary swelling of the wood; simple lubrication with paraffin, candle wax, or special silicone lubricants may take care of this. Remove the drawer, wipe dust from edges and guide strips on which the drawer rides. Apply lubricant to guides *and* to edges.

If a drawer opens only partially, put a trouble light (in a wire cage), screwed into an extension-cord socket, in the drawer. This should dry the wood out sufficiently to release the drawer.

If the above doesn't solve the problem, sanding may be required to shave down the edges. Find out where the drawer is sticking. Inspect the drawer and the guides. Points of contact usually show as dark, polished areas along the edges. Sand down these spots with medium-grade sandpaper. Try the drawer frequently, remove only as much wood as necessary. If the drawer sides are too high, sand on the top edge rather than the bottom.

Sticking drawers might possibly be the fault of an uneven floor. This can be checked out with a carpenter's level; the chest top should be absolutely level and the sides vertical. If not level, use thin strips of wood or cardboard as wedges under the low side. As you add wedges, check the level to make sure the chest is balanced from side to side, back to front.

Loose Veneer Sections

Edges around tabletops, desks, etc., that have split loose can easily be glued back together again. Wedge the split open just enough to work glue into the crevice and on both edges of split portion. Press sections together; apply pressure with clamps or by wrapping tightly with heavy tape. If using clamps, protect wood finish by padding with cardboard.

Refinishing A Table

The basic techniques explained here can be applied to almost any refinishing job as you become experienced.

The quickest way to remove the old finish is with a liquid or paste chemical paint remover, which softens the old finish so it can be easily scraped off with a putty knife. Liquid remover is the least expensive, but it tends to run off vertical surfaces before it has a chance to do its job. It also evaporates quickly, often requiring additional applications. Paste remover stays in place on vertical surfaces and works longer by retaining its moisture. There is also a water-wash type, liquid or paste, that enables you to simply wash the softened finish away, thus making it especially convenient when working in carved and intricate areas that are difficult to reach with a scraper.

An important consideration with paint remover is its flammability; check the information on the container or consult your dealer for a safe, nonflammable type.

Regardless of the type you choose, use the paint remover in a well-ventilated room, never near fire or flame. Don't smoke. Wear old clothes; protect your hands and skin by wearing gloves and a long-sleeved shirt. Cover the floor with newspapers; set legs of table in empty coffee cans to catch drippings. (Remover can be saved and reused later.)

Apply remover with a clean paintbrush, using the side of the brush rather than the tip. Spread thickly with a single stroke. Move in the direction of the grain; don't brush back and forth, as this can break the surface seal that prevents evaporation. Use short strokes, refilling the brush frequently; touch up missed spots with more remover rather than trying to spread the amount already applied. Now let the remover work, which usually requires between ten and 30 minutes. When old finish has softened, scrape off residue with a putty knife. If patches of old finish remain, reapply remover and repeat process. Scrape residue into an old can for easy disposal. To remove finish on carved or grooved areas, use a stiff toothbrush or wire-bristled suede brush. Directions on paint-remover container will tell you whether or not to wash the surface before sanding.

Although it is the most tedious part of the refinishing process, there is no substitute for careful sanding. Use a rubber or cork sanding block (or make your own by pasting felt to a small piece of wood and folding the sandpaper over it). For intricate areas, use a small square of sandpaper held lightly under your finger. When working on a fairly large surface, save time and effort by renting a power sander (the belt sander or orbital sander are recommended). However you sand, always work in the direction of the wood's grain. Don't bear down on any one spot but keep the movement even, being careful not to let the sandpaper rock over the edges, thus rounding off the corners. When the surface is smooth to touch, wipe away all traces of sandpaper dust with a tack cloth (this is a varnish-impregnated cloth).

There are any number of possibilities for the new finish—natural, bleached, enameled or antiqued—but we've elected to use a stain. In selecting a stain, remember that each one is designed for a specific wood; for example, if a piece of furniture is oak, you shouldn't use mahogany or walnut or maple. With pine, however, you can use any stain you prefer. Wood stains carry such names as light walnut, dark walnut, red mahogany, maple, light oak, and so on. The approximate colors are usually on display in color chips or stained-wood samples to help in the selection.

Following the grain, brush on stain freely or wipe on with a clean, lint-free cloth; let penetrate for about 15 minutes; wipe off surplus across the grain, then wipe with the grain to eliminate streaks. The amount of time you leave the stain on will determine the final color (the longer stain penetrates, the deeper the color). If not dark enough after stain has been wiped off, repeat process. When satisfied, wipe clean; the color should be in the pores and fibers of the wood and not on the surface. Let dry 24 to 48 hours before applying finish.

The three most popular materials to choose from for the final finish are shellac, lacquer and varnish. Consult your paint dealer about your choice; directions will be on the container. For the sake of brevity here, we've selected a spray-on-lacquer finish. It's durable and dries rapidly, an advantage since many thin coats are necessary. Hold the can about 12 inches away from the surface, and with a steady up-and-down motion spray on the lacquer in a fine, light mist. Let finish dry overnight. Sand the surface with fine sandpaper. For a hard surface finish, repeat the process three or four times. Finally, rub on paste wax, let dry and polish to a luster.

What to Do When Your Books Are Crowding You Out

Why spend up to $100 or more for a new bookcase when you can build one yourself for only about $20? We've made ours of three-quarter-inch birch plywood; it stands 36 inches high, is 30 inches wide and 10 inches deep. You can obviously vary this size or use different woods but our $20 estimate is based on the design below.

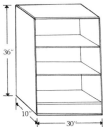

First, to make your job easier, have the wood cut to size. You'll need:
1 top—10″ x 30″
2 uprights—10″ x 35¼″
3 shelves—10″ x 28½″
1 bottom strip—3″ x 28½″
Ask your lumber dealer if he can give the lumber a preliminary sanding; it may cost extra but is worth the small price.

Also order: ½ pound 2-inch finishing nails, 2 sheets coarse sandpaper, and 2 sheets fine sandpaper. If you'd rather put the bookcase together with screws, get a box of 1¾ number 9 wood screws.

Assemble tools: hammer, screwdriver, pencil, spirit level, ruler or yardstick, and work gloves.

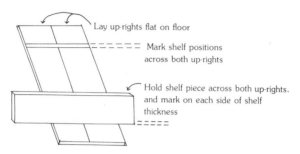

Lay up-rights flat on floor

Mark shelf positions across both up-rights

Hold shelf piece across both up-rights. and mark on each side of shelf thickness

To begin: lay the uprights side by side on the floor, flat side down, and align ends. Set one shelf on edge across both boards and mark where each shelf is to go (the bottom shelf must be three inches from the floor; the others can be any distance apart you wish) by making a pencil mark on each side of shelf thickness all the way across both pieces. Be sure all lines are straight; measure to be sure both ends of pencil mark are the same distance from end of board. Turn *one* upright over and extend shelf marking onto it. Turn other upright over and repeat markings. It is between these guidelines that you will set shelves and drive nails.

To fasten shelves to uprights: lay one upright across a support (a box, the step of a ladder, a sturdy chair back, or low table) and adjust height of support to 28½". Slide one shelf into position

under the horizontal upright between penciled guidelines. Nail through side piece and into shelf from above, using three nails in each shelf end. Nail in remaining shelves, shifting supports as needed to maintain balance and rigidity.

Turn the unit over and lay the other upright over the up-reaching shelf-ends. (Push the whole thing into a corner to brace it a bit). Align all edges and sides within penciled guidelines by tapping pieces into position with a hammer. Use the level to check for accuracy. Then nail from above as before.

Turn the bookcase into the upright position and nail on the top piece. Next, turn the unit on its side and slip bottom strip into position; drive two nails in from above. Turn bookcase over and nail other end of strip the same way.

Note: If using screws instead of nails, assemble as above but drill holes first with an electric drill. To assure getting the holes straight, hold the shelf pieces in position with partially driven nails, which can be removed later.

Sand the unit with coarse sandpaper and dust with damp cloth or sponge. To paint or stain the bookcase, sand again with fine sandpaper (which should also erase pencil marks). Use nozzle attachment of vacuum cleaner to get wood dust out of corners. Dust again with damp cloth or sponge. Brush on wood primer; let dry, then paint. If using stain, apply then seal. Some products seal and stain at the same time—your hardware store or lumber dealer can advise you.

Framing & Hanging Pictures

Pictures are an important part of a home s personality. Whether yours are original paintings or inexpensive prints, posters, photographs or maps, the way in which they are framed is important if you want to bring out their best.

It is possible to do the job yourself—and save a considerable amount of money. Large art-supply stores are a good source for the parts you'll need. They carry frames of various sizes, in finished or unfinished wood, in designs ranging from plain to intricate. Some frames come packaged in sections ready for snap-together assembly; these come in varying sizes and have anodized finishes of aluminum or gold, or acrylic finishes in many colors. Also available are kits that contain a sheet of acrylic plastic (to serve in place of glass), a mat board and rigid backing board; these too come in many sizes and are designed to fit smoothly into the sectioned frames. In some stores you will find precut mats, and some art-supply and framing stores will cut mats and glass to your exact specification.

Framing

A frame should suit its picture: A traditional design is best for classical subjects, a provincial design for a still life, and a contemporary design for bold modern or abstract pieces. The frame's size is also important: Fragile-looking pictures need frames about a half inch wide, medium pictures can use a frame up to two inches wide, and very strong ones need bold, wider frames. Paintings on canvas or board, in oil or acrylic, usually require a frame only, but pictures on paper need the protection of glass.

The mat separates the picture from direct contact with the glass. It's simply a piece of artists' board, cut out in the center to form a border for the picture. Oil paintings and other art that have strong, bright colors don't require matting. The width of the mat is determined by the size, style and colors of the picture; a border of at least two to three inches is most often recommended. As for the color of the mat, white or off-white is usually the safest. If a colored mat is selected, it should be a color from the picture's background. The mat's texture should harmonize with the picture: Coarse-textured mats are best for strong, large pictures, smooth mats for small, delicate prints. If you don't feel confident about cutting a mat yourself, give the store the dimensions and they'll cut it for you. But for the really brave, measure and cut with a ruler and mat knife, utility cutter or razor blade.

Backing, which finishes off the picture, should be rag board followed by a layer of chipboard (a closely compacted cardboard). Because a print may shift in its frame, it is often anchored to the top of the backing with regular paper glue. When all of these layers have been placed together, finish framing by sealing the back with a piece of brown paper (glue it in place).

Finally, attach screw eyes and picture wire to the frame (unless it already has an attachment for hanging). Screw eyes (which come in various sizes to support different weights) and braided picture wire are available at variety, art-supply and hardware stores. Attach one screw eye to each side of the frame back, at a spot no more than one quarter to one third of the way down from the top of the frame; this placement prevents the picture from slanting too far forward when hung. If necessary, start holes for the screws with a sharp-pointed instrument, then work in screws by hand; use pliers for tightening, if necessary. The picture wire should be long enough so that the center reaches halfway to the top of the frame after each end has been threaded through a screw eye and twisted back around the supporting wire for about an inch of length.

Hanging

How the picture is hung depends on its size and weight. Picture hooks, which are sold in packages marked with the maximum weight each hook will hold, come with nails that are driven into the wall at an angle. Adhesive hooks and mounts that stick without nails may also be used, but only for small, lightweight pictures. For a brick or concrete wall, drill a hole and insert a masonry nail or screw.

There are several ways of determining where to place the hook on the wall. For a lightweight picture, place your index finger under the center of the wire and hold it taut; place the picture against the wall and lightly mark the spot your finger touches with a pencil (this will be where the wire and hook meet, not where the nail is driven, so judge accordingly when driving the nail). For heavier and bulkier pictures, measure the distance from the uppermost point of the taut wire to the top of the frame; hold the picture to the wall and have someone mark where the middle of the top of the frame will be; from there measure down to where the wire should meet the hook.

Give a Face-lift to Summer Furniture

Give outdoor furniture a new lease on life for summer. Here, the major problems and what you can do about them.

Redwood

If a board is badly cracked or split, pry it apart gently and very slightly with a knife; work in waterproof glue. Reinforce with clamps, if possible.

Redwood furniture usually has a clear finish. At least once a year, it needs a coat of redwood sealer, underside as well as top. This seals the wood against moisture, dirt, and stains while restoring the original color of the wood.

Redwood furniture may need to be refinished. Apply a water-rinse paint remover to remove the old finish; then rinse with clear water, and allow to dry thoroughly. Since redwood is a soft wood that dents and scratches easily, sand away surface stains or marks with very fine sandpaper. To bring the redwood back to its natural color, apply several layers of clear or lightly tinted wood stain, a waterproof penetrating finish, or a redwood preservative.

Wrought Iron

Hose off, or wash with suds, and rinse. Retouch any nicks or chips with paint to prevent rusting. If the paint is in good condition and only needs renewing, rub the finish with steel wool or sandpaper. Then wipe clean with a cloth dampened in paint thinner; allow to dry, and apply one or two coats of outdoor enamel.

If the finish is in poor condition (cracked or peeling), remove it with steel wool or a stiff brush. Remove all traces of rust with medium steel wool or sandpaper. Next, wash the metal with a commercial metal conditioner that contains phosphoric acid. (Be sure to wear rubber gloves.) Rinse the acid away, and dry. Coat with metal primer; when dry, apply two coats of outdoor enamel to the spots you have worked on. Finish by coating entire piece with two coats of the same enamel.

For general maintenance, apply a metal-wax coating twice a year. In coastal areas, clean frequently to prevent salt deposits.

Aluminum

Even though aluminum is rust-resistant, the frames of chairs and tables can become dull, pitted, and dirty. Remove dust and dirt with a stiff brush and damp cloth. To polish the frames, use detergent-based steel-wool pads. Rinse quickly, and remove residue with a dry cloth. Use auto-paste wax on the clean frames to restore luster.

To remove bad discolorations, wash with phosphoric-acid metal conditioner (as with wrought iron). Rinse, and polish the metal with fine-grade steel wool. Wipe clean with a paint thinner; then coat with a clear, nonyellowing acrylic lacquer.

Wicker and Rattan

This furniture absorbs dirt easily, and also tends to fade. Vacuum thoroughly to remove dust; scrub with a brush, warm water, and detergent; then rinse, and dry thoroughly. Sprayed with a coat of clear varnish, it will look like new.

If a piece is badly stained, spray with outdoor enamel. Before painting or varnishing, repair loose or broken strands with waterproof glue. Tack into place with rustproof nails.

Plastic Webbing, Cushions, Canvas

Several times a season, wash plastic webbing with detergent suds, and rinse with a hose. Wipe dry. If webbing is worn and frayed, replace it. A ready-made seat or back may be available in exactly the right size. If not, purchase the plastic material by the yard, and cut it to fit, using the old seat or back as a pattern. Fasten new seat or back to the framework of wooden chairs with staples or tacks. Fasten to metal chairs with sheet-metal screws.

Plastic or canvas cushions and seats should be scrubbed with a brush and detergent suds, and rinsed and dried thoroughly. If there are rips, tears, or holes, patch them with matching material, using fabric cement. Ripped seams may be mended with heavy cord.

If plastic or canvas is badly faded, restore with fabric coating. It comes in many colors. Use the aerosol spray for plastic, the brush-on kind for canvas.

How to Maintain the Life and Luster of Home Furnishings

The home that takes care of itself is not yet a reality. Even with today's easy-care finishes and materials, time and devotion are called for to keep your home in tip-top shape. If you continually practice preventive maintenance, then you've taken a giant step toward extending the life of your home furnishings and saving yourself the bother and expense of excessive repairs. Here are some timely tips to aid you in preventive maintenance

Carpeting

The extra attention shown to your rugs and carpeting pays off in their enhanced appearance and longer life. Proper carpet care includes vacuuming, probably once a week (more often for those heavily trafficked areas), to remove surface dirt and get at that heavy grit that sinks deep into the pile. In between these thorough vacuumings, attention should be paid to surface dirt immediately after a mishap.

When vacuuming, don't try to find short cuts—move the furniture to get at those places where dirt accumulates—the dust that settles on a rug under furniture can be harmful to the fiber and cause discolorations in the carpet's hue. You should apply five or six forward and backward strokes in heavily trafficked areas, and three strokes elsewhere. Deeply carved rugs or carpets demand more strokes for a thorough cleaning. If the carpet has a directional lay, be careful to make your final stroke in the same direction as the lay of the pile. Shaggy rugs demand more than shabby attention—special care here means extra vacuuming before the dirt becomes embedded in the shag. Some vacuum cleaners come equipped with a special shag attachment or an adjustment geared especially for this type of carpet. Shag pile tends to flatten and mat when it's walked on; vacuuming will help to restore the fluff of the shag. Also on the market is a device called a shag rake, which fluffs the shag and keeps it from matting. But what a shag rake doesn't do is pick up the grit lodged in between the strands; so don't forget to vacuum at the same time. Wall-to-wall carpet also makes exclusive demands—special attention should be paid to those areas that edge the room; the crevice tool of the vacuum is ideal for this task.

Furniture can crush carpet pile. Preventive maintenance here calls for holding a steam iron several inches above these depressions in the carpet and moving it back and forth in order to perk up the pile. If possible, rugs should be turned from time to time to prevent undo wear in those areas most often under foot. Use rug padding to increase the life of the rug, to add softness, and absorb noise. Don't place lamp cords under rugs; they cause extra wear and may present a safety hazard.

When vacuuming no longer seems to restore the color and luster of carpeting, it's time for a shampoo; about once yearly is recommended. (Professional cleaning every few years is also part of the program.) Thorough cleaning can be accomplished with a brush and a powder cleaner or a rug shampoo and an electric rug shampooer (you can rent one of these). New spray foam cleaners are now on the market that make shampooing a snap; they're quick, and offer fast drying. Don't apply too much cleaner, you don't want to soak the rug backing. Heavily soiled areas may require a double application. If your rug is not completely dry when the time comes to replace the furniture, spread squares of wax paper under furniture legs to guard against staining.

Spills on rugs shouldn't be allowed to settle. Blot, don't rub; use an absorbent material such as paper towels or facial tissues to pick up the spills. Remove greasy spills with a solvent such as dry-cleaning fluid. Water soluble stains—coffee, ice-cream, chocolate, egg, etc.—should be attacked with a small dose of rug shampoo foam, or the suds from a solution of detergent and water. When spot-cleaning carpets, work from the edge of the stain toward the center, constantly turning the cloth to expose a clean surface.

Upholstery

A weekly cleaning does wonders for upholstery. Regular care means that no spill or stain goes unattended, that a shampoo be administered whenever necessary, and that an energetic vacuuming be performed upon upholstery (using the upholstery brush-attachment of your vacuum and a crevice tool to get deep into corners) at least once a week. Extra loving care means not forgetting to vacuum the outside back of chairs and sofas and an occasional turning of the cushions to make sure the filling remains evenly distributed. Be gentle with your upholstery—don't use a stiff-bristled brush that could damage delicate fibers—and keep your furniture out of direct sunlight to prevent it from fading.

Spot Removal: Keep the tools of the trade at hand—a stain chart, upholstery shampoo, and a good spot remover are musts. If your ice cream drips onto the couch or your coffee cascades onto a cushion, immediately blot the excess stain with a paper towel or facial tissue. Absorbent powders such as cornstarch and commercial spot removers are ideal for conquering fresh grease spots. Dry cleaning fluids also remove these greasy stains too, but they shouldn't be used on furniture padded with foam rubber; instead try a foamy upholstery cleaner. Many food stains will vanish under the suds of a simple solution composed of detergent and warm water.

Whatever means you use toward the end of removing stains, be especially sure to pre-test the fabric for colorfastness. This simple test should take place in an inconspicuous spot on your furniture. Use cool or luke-warm water, never hot. Apply the cleaner sparingly unless otherwise recommended. Work your magic from the edge of the stain in toward its center; and blot, don't rub. The faster the material drys after cleaning the better; a hair dryer or fan is helpful here.

Shampooing: Overwetness is what to watch out for when shampooing your upholstery. For synthetic fibers and cottons, a light duty detergent-foam or upholstery shampoo does the trick. These shampoos dry into hard crystals which pick up easily with a light vacuuming. If you feature plastic upholstery on your furniture, a mild detergent and water solution is suggested. If leather is your thing, saddle soap; paste wax; leather preservative; or upholstery shampoo is the thing to use to keep it beautiful. Upholstery shampoo is recommended also for fabrics that harbor foam rubber padding—a solvent solution could damage the foam. To clean woven upholstery worry-free, foam cleaners should be used; a liquid might discolor the fabric if it seeps into the back of the upholstery.

Draperies

Don't let your draperies become a cover-up for dirt. The subtle folds in the fabric are there to be beautiful, not to provide lodgings for dust that can weaken the fibers in the fabric. A regular dusting with a vacuum dusting-brush or an upholstery brush is called for. If you're careful to keep them dust free, your draperies won't demand frequent washings or stints at the dry cleaner's. If your draperies appear at a window that gets exceptional sun or features a southern exposure, be sure to line them to protect the fabric from fading.

Venetian Blinds

Venetian blinds are notorious catchalls for dust, and you should attend to their needs accordingly. The more often you go over the slats with the dusting-brush attachment on your vacuum, the less often the blinds will cry out for a good washing. For a special measure of preventive maintenance apply a cleaning or dusting wax after washing and watch how easily the dust will flick off in the future.

Wood Paneling

A regular dusting will distinguish your wood paneling by maintaining the beauty and luster of the wood. Once again, the vacuum cleaner dusting-brush should play a large part in your maintenance program, but a large dustcloth wrapped around a long-handled brush, wax applier, or broom works wonders too. Additionally, there are specifically formulated cleaners for wood paneling that both clean and protect. They hide scratches and blemishes and help repel dust particles so that dusting is required less frequently.

Wood Furniture

Wood thrives on care, not neglect. Dusting is one of those dastardly jobs that ultimately saves you from the drudgeries of more formidable chores; dusting removes film and gritty dirt *before* it can scratch the furniture's surface and literally rob it of its sheen. Use a dustcloth that is soft, absorbent, and clean—cotton knitwear, flannel scraps, or even old diapers will work beautifully. A dusting wax used along with your cloth saves the wood from scratches, as well as increasing its dust-absorbing power. (There are pre-treated dusting cloths available.)

A thorough cleaning of wood furniture is called for when the surface begins to be marred with sticky stains and greasy finger prints. Use a cleaning wax that is designed to cope with common household soil while it removes previous coats of wax or polish. (Washing with detergent and water is not recommended.) Saturate a cloth with wax; or, if you prefer to use a spray cleaner apply the wax directly to the furniture's surface being sure to wet it thoroughly. Clean a square foot at a time using a circular motion; your final wipe should be directed with the grain. With a second clean cloth wipe the area dry while the wax is still moist; if the cloth becomes too damp to wipe it dry, use a fresh one. After cleaning, apply a furniture wax according to label directions.

Hard Surface Floors

Hard floors come in an extensive variety of materials—wood; cork; vinyl; asphalt; ceramic tile; quarry tile; slate; and flagstone. Whatever the material covering your floor, you can be sure of one thing—your floor takes a lot of abuse. To keep floors beautiful it's necessary to lavish upon them care and protection; but it's also important not to overclean or wax them excessively. If you offer daily care and polish them regularly (only if you have a type of floor that requires it), floors should need a thorough cleaning only two or three times a year—except in heavily trafficked zones like the kitchen and hallway.

Curb the impulse to wax your floor to the point there's more wax than floor—a waxing is called for only when it begins to look dull and does not regain its sheen when buffed. Two thin coats of wax are better than one thick one. When using cleaning wax, polish with an electric polisher, then buff to a hard finish. If the floor appears slippery it hasn't been buffed enough. Vacuum or dry mop wood floors and damp mop others regularly, so that you won't walk dust and dirt into the wax and dull the luster.

If you intend to use one of the new one-step cleaners that both clean and shine while you damp mop, be careful that any old layers of buffable-wax are removed from the floor. Between waxings, keep floors looking fantastic: buff them with an electric polisher; rewax the areas most under foot frequently; damp mop between scrubbings to remove spills or dirty tracks; and remove those ugly black scuff marks made by rubber heels and casters (this can be accomplished by rubbing them gently with fine dry steel wool that has been dipped in wax—solvent-based for everything but asphalt floors [a water-based wax is needed for this latter type]—then repolish the spots).

Some sheet floorings have a special-wear surface that shines without waxing; in fact, you shouldn't wax it at all, as wax won't even stick to the surface. Occasionally sweep and damp mop them. If cleaning with an all-purpose cleaner or detergent be sure to thoroughly rinse the floor even if label says this is unnecessary. Don't use steel wool or scouring cleansers on these floors. If they seem abnormally dull, especially in the heavily trafficked areas, a special finish is available that restores their shine.

Wood and sealed cork floors should be cleaned with a solvent-based polishing or self-polishing wax; asphalt with a water-based wax. Either solvent- or water-based waxes are also recommended for vinyl, ceramic, brick, slate, and flagstone floors.

Door Troubles

If a door is sticking, it could be as simple as one or two loose screws in the hinges. Open the door wide and tighten each screw. If the screws just go around and won't tighten, this means the hole is so worn that the screws have nothing to bite into. Remove screws and fill holes with wooden plugs that have been dipped in glue; or, more simply, use wooden kitchen matches (with heads removed). Then reinsert the original screws and tighten.

If this doesn't solve the problem, then you need to determine exactly where the sticking occurs. This can be done by running a sheet of heavy paper or thin cardboard around the edges of the closed door. The paper should slide freely; where it bunches or sticks is the trouble spot. If the door sticks along the bottom, the bottom hinge may be recessed too deeply into the doorframe; or the upper hinge might not be set in far enough. To correct this, bring out bottom hinge by placing a piece of cardboard (a shim) behind hinge leaf. To install cardboard shim, unscrew the hinge leaf with the door in an open position and propped up. Cut the cardboard slightly smaller than the hinge leaf and slip behind it; screw hinge back in place. Additional thicknesses of cardboard may be added if necessary. If the door still sticks at the bottom, it may be necessary to shave a small amount of wood from the outside edge of the door where rubbing occurs. This can usually be done by using coarse sandpaper wrapped around a block of wood, or by applying a sheet of sandpaper to the doorframe and opening and closing the door on it until enough has been shaved away to prevent sticking. If the rubbing and sticking occur at the top of the door, the trouble lies with the upper hinge.

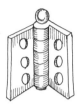

When doors resist closing or spring back open unless they're slammed *hard*, shimming out the hinges is again the remedy—but in a somewhat different way. Narrow cardboard shims, half the width of the hinge leaf, should be placed under the back half of the hinge leaf (near the pin). This tilts the hinge more into the door opening so it closes without binding. Prop the door open as before, loosen hinge screws, slip strips of cardboard under back edges of the hinges and replace screws.

If the door sticks along the edge, planing or trimming is the solution. If only one or two spots are the problem, hand planing can usually be done without having to take the door off. But if it needs to be planed along its entire length, or if it rubs next to the door latch, the door will have to be taken down to do the job properly. To remove door, tap out the hinge pins with a hammer and screwdriver, then lift it off. Rather than planing the door along the lock side (which would necessitate removing the lock), plane along the back edge; it's far easier to remove the hinge leaves. If necessary, the recesses in which the hinges sit can be deepened by cutting them out with a chisel.

If bottom edge of the door rubs along its entire width, remove the door and plane the bottom. If a door won't stay closed because the latch bolt doesn't engage the strike-plate opening on doorframe, the opening is probably not lined up with the latch bolt. You can move the strike plate a fraction of an inch higher or lower, or it may be taken off and the opening filed slightly larger. If necessary, strike plate may be moved closer to the door edge by shimming out behind it with one or more pieces of cardboard.

Fixing Windows That Stick

Windows that stick or won't open or close properly are a great annoyance. The trouble may be caused by dampness, which makes the wood swell, or by a careless paint job, in which paint was allowed to harden around the window. Solutions to these problems are quite easy.

Double-hung windows that are stiff and difficult to open and close can usually be loosened with simple lubrication. Rub a block of paraffin or even a heavy candle on the inside of the vertical tracks to improve the sliding action. Squirts of a silicone lubricant spray will also do the trick; this works particularly well on windows with metal stripping in the channels.

If the window has sash cords, the pulley over which these cords run may need attention. Expose the pulley on each side at the top of the frame by pulling down the upper sash. Apply a drop of lubricating oil on each pulley shaft on both sides of the wheel. Graphite dust, which is sold for lock lubrication, also works well. If the sash cords are broken or badly stretched, they should be replaced, preferably with metal sash chains. You may want to call in a professional for this job, however, since it involves removing the molding.

If a window sticks because the wood has swollen from moisture absorption, there is a simple cure if the condition is not too
severe. With a wooden block and hammer, tap the top molding
(the strip along the window frame) inward. Then raise the window
sash all the way up and place the block against the outside edge
of the stop molding (the edge that is against the sash when the
window is closed). Hit the block hard with the hammer, working
up and down entire length of the molding on both sides of the
frame. If this procedure doesn't loosen the window, remove the
entire stop molding by prying it off with a chisel. Trim the edge of
the stop molding slightly with some fine sandpaper to provide
clearance, and renail the molding into place.

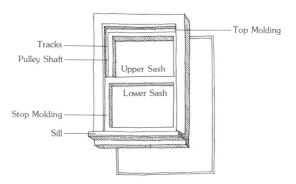

Top Molding

Tracks

Pulley Shaft

Upper Sash

Lower Sash

Stop Molding

Sill

If the window is stuck shut because of hardened paint, force a
stiff putty knife between the edge of the sash and the stop molding. Tap the blade in with a hammer, slightly twisting the handle
of the knife to provide a prying action; this should help to break
the sash free. Pry along both sides of the sash as well as along
the sill at the bottom of the sash until the window can be raised.
In more severe cases, you may have to pry it open from the
bottom, working from the outside of the window. Use a hatchet
for this, tapping its head with a hammer into the crack where the
bottom of the sash meets the windowsill. Moving the hatchet
along the width of the window, lift gently as you go along until the

sash comes free. When you can raise the window, scrape paint from the outside edge of the stop molding with a wood chisel, being careful not to chip or gouge the wood. Smooth stop molding with a piece of fine sandpaper wrapped around a block of wood.

Casement windows also present problems when their hinges and edges get rusty, when the track underneath the sash is clogged with dust and dirt or when the handle assembly becomes stiff. To prevent rust on a steel casement's hinges and edges, you should paint them periodically with an exterior trim paint or enamel. Scrape rusty areas clean to the bare metal, and touch up with a rust-resistant metal primer. Allow this to dry before applying paint. About once a year, oil the hinges; do this when the window is slightly open, and then again when it's open all the way, to insure uniform penetration. Clean out the track underneath the sash with a wire brush to remove rust and dirt, and then apply a liberal amount of lubricating spray in the groove. If the handle or crank that opens the window is hard to turn, try a few drops of oil in the joint where the handle enters its case. If this does not help, the handle mechanism may have to be removed, any hardened lubricant cleaned out with kerosene or a similar solvent and fresh lubricant applied.

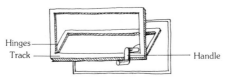

Aluminum casement or sliding windows usually don't need paint for protection, but their grooves may need to be cleaned out once a year or so and a paste wax applied to keep them moving smoothly. If the frames are pitted, rub them lightly with steel wool before applying paste wax.

Replacing Broken Window Glass

A broken windowpane is almost inevitable at some point, especially if there are active children around. Repairing broken glass is an easy job but one that requires very cautious handling.

To remove the broken glass, it's wise to wear heavy gloves or use pliers to prevent cutting your fingers. Gently pull pieces out in sections as large as possible. If a piece is stuck with hardened putty, move it back and forth gently; then pull straight out. If there are really stubborn chips of glass in the corners, use a hammer and chisel to gently knock them out. To prevent further handling, it's a good idea to have a carton by your side to discard the broken pieces.

When you have taken out all of the glass, the hardened putty that surrounded it must also be removed. Scrape it out with a narrow chisel or screwdriver; for the really bad spots, you can carefully tap the chisel with a hammer.

As you remove the putty, pull out the glazier's points with pliers. These points are tiny triangular pieces of flat metal that hold the glass in place (new points will be needed later). If you are working on a metal sash, there will be spring clips or tension strips that can be pried out with a screwdriver and reused later if they are in good condition.

When all putty has been removed, clean out the groove thoroughly; then paint with a coating of linseed oil, wood preservative or latex house paint; dry thoroughly. For metal frames apply a coat of paste wax and allow to dry. This priming is important because it seals the frame opening against moisture and insures a good bond later.

Measure the length and width of the opening and have new glass cut $\frac{1}{8}$ inch smaller in each dimension. (Your hardware dealer has a special machine that does this job accurately.) Apply a thin layer of putty or glazing compound in the groove around the frame to cushion the glass. Carefully press the new glass into the compound. For a wooden frame, lay glazier's points against the glass and carefully tap into the frame around the four sides. (You can tap these in at no risk to the glass by placing a screwdriver against flat side of point and tapping hammer against screwdriver.) Depending on the size of the glass pane, anywhere from two to four points for each side may be needed. With a metal frame, special spring clips are used that fit into holes in the frame and press against the edge of the glass. Some types of metal frames use plastic tension strips, which are pressed into place with a screwdriver. If you had these on your metal frames and removed them without damage, they may be reused.

Now you are ready to seal with putty or a glazing compound. Roll the compound into pencil-size strips, lay the strips into the groove around the edge of the sash, and press into position with a putty knife. Smooth it to form a triangular-shape bevel between the sash and the glass. Cut off excess glazing material with the corner of the putty knife. Smudges on the glass can be removed after they have dried for a couple of days by wiping with turpentine. Let dry for a couple of weeks; then apply paint to the glazing compound to match the color of the window frame. The paint should extend slightly onto the glass to assure a secure, weathertight seal.

Repairing Window Screens

Even an attractive house will lose its inviting appearance if the window screens are punctured, torn from their frames or split because of rust and corrosion. Fortunately, screens are both simple and inexpensive to repair. Screening fabric is available in rolls or in patches for both major and minor repairs. You may also patch a screen with a scrap of matching wire mesh if the scrap is in good condition.

To Patch

Cut a rectangular opening in the damaged screen just slightly larger than the puncture or tear. Cut a new rectangular screening patch two inches larger than the trimmed hole. Remove the three outside wires on all four sides of the patch to make raveled edges of about one half inch. Bend the ends of these wires over a block or edge of a ruler to form prongs that will secure the patch to the screen. Place the patch over the hole from the outside, and push prongs through the screen. On the inside, bend down the ends of the wires toward the center of the hole. It helps to have someone on the outside to press against the patch while you are working from the inside.

In the case of very small holes, these can be mended by stitching back and forth with a fine wire and a large darning needle.

To Cover A Wooden-Framed Screen

Pry off the moldings, being very careful not to damage them as they will have to be reused. Remove old tacks, staples and screen wire. Cut new screen mesh to size, allowing an extra half inch of material on all sides beyond the outside of the molding. This makes a hem that will be folded under the molding to insure a better grip when stapling or nailing. A staple gun is the speediest tool as it requires only one hand for fastening while the other hand stretches the screen. Starting on one long side, tack or staple the mesh into each corner and allow the excess half inch to extend out beyond the molding. Fold over the excess material, and tack or staple through the double thickness at one-inch intervals, beginning in the center. Keep material stretched tightly to avoid bunching. Repeat on the other long side of the screen. When both long sides are secure, fasten screening in the same manner to one of the short ends of the screen, then to the other, making sure the mesh is pulled tight in all directions. Replace molding over edges of screening.

For Metal Frames

With metal frames the wire mesh is held in place with a plastic bedding strip, or spline, that fits into the groove around the edge of the screen frame and is pressed down on top of the screening so that the mesh is clamped tightly into the spline groove. No tacks or staples are needed. Begin the replacement by laying the frame flat on a table. Then pry out the existing plastic spline, and pull out the old screen wire. Cut the new screening so that it is as large as the outer side of the screen frame. Lay screening over top of frame. Trim off corners at a 45-degree angle, making sure that the line of cut leaves enough material in each corner to reach into the spline groove. Lay the spline for one of the long sides on top of the screening, and use a thick-bladed screwdriver to tap the spline into its groove. Repeat on the opposite long side, pulling the mesh tight as the spline is forced into its groove. Tap the splines into place in the same manner on the short sides. Trim off the excess screening material with a sharp knife or razor blade on the outside of the spline. Return the window or door screens to their original locations and enjoy insect-free ventilation.

To Replace Damaged Screens

If the screen is torn in several places, or if it is badly corroded, it will have to be replaced. There are different kinds of metal and plastic screening material, but one of the easiest to install is fiber glass. It won't crease or dent, is easy to stretch tight by hand, cuts easily with household scissors and, once installed, won't corrode, stretch or shrink.

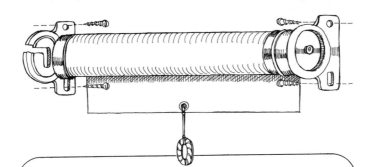

Putting Window Shades in Their Place

It's all too easy to let your window shades get out of control. How many do you know that jerk up or droop down or just hang around limply—and get away with it because the people of the house shrink fearfully from installing new ones? It's too bad, because the job isn't all that formidable. All you need is some basic information, and we provide it here.

First to the basic bracket types: *Inside brackets* are the kind to use whenever there is enough depth inside the window frame to accommodate the roller; shade then pulls down from back of roller. *Reverse brackets* allow the shade to be pulled down in front of the roller; they also allow extra clearance if the window depth is shallow. *Inside extension brackets* are mounted inside the window frame but extend slightly into the room; they're also used on narrow frames and to extend the shade to clear casement-window cranks, hinged jalousie windows, and so on. *Outside brackets* are mounted on window trim or the plaster adjacent to the window. They're used for shades wider than the window (to shut out light that creeps in at the sides or to give the illusion of a wider window), or for bottom-up shades that install at sill or floor level and operate on pulley cords (they're for cathedral-type windows, skylights, or to insure privacy while still letting in light from the top). *Combination brackets* accommodate both a window shade and a curtain rod. *Ceiling brackets* are especially useful for windows that are ceiling-high or deeply recessed. *Double brackets* are used for installation of two shades at the same window (usually one's translucent, the other a room darkener). A word about windows in aluminum frames: Because it is impossible to install brackets on aluminum, you would have to use outside brackets mounted on the wall or, if possible, ceiling brackets. If aluminum windows are set in wood trim, use inside or extension brackets.

Once you know the brackets you want to use, you're ready to measure for the shades. Accurate measurements are essential—if you miss by even half an inch, your new shades won't fit. Use only a wood or metal ruler—cloth tapes or string may stretch and throw off calculations.

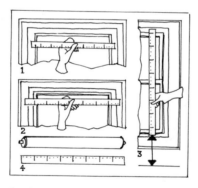

To determine shade width needed, measure the exact distance between the points where brackets are to be installed. Though windows may seem to be identical in width, always measure each window. When ordering, indicate the exact measurement and the particular mounting being used. For inside brackets, measure from one inside surface of window frame to the opposite inside surface (see diagram 1). For outside brackets, ceiling brackets and brackets for bottom-up installation, mark the position where brackets will be placed and measure distance between (2); for these mountings, it is recommended that the shades overlap the window frame 1½ to 2 inches on each side. For length, measure the full height of your window opening from top frame to lower sill and then add 12 inches for roll-over (3).

To replace shades, measure old rollers from tip to tip, *including* the metal pins that fit into the brackets (4); specify tip-to-tip measurement on your order. Since rollers loosen and eventually wear out, it is wise to get new ones when you get new shades. For unusually wide—and more expensive—rollers, some stores will attach new shades to old rollers.

Hints for installation: To determine exactly where to put the brackets, hold up the rolled shade and mark the bracket position; allow enough distance from top and back of window frame so that roll will turn freely.

Mount brackets with screws, not nails; nails are likely to work loose.

When putting up new shades that are wrapped in paper or plastic, tear just a bit of the wrapping from each end of shade, leaving the rest intact so that shade won't unroll or be soiled by finger marks while you're working.

Be certain the flat tip of the roller mechanism is vertical in the slot hole of the bracket.

Never oil the mechanism of a shade roller.

Some simple repairs: If spring is too tight, roll shade up to the top and remove it from its brackets; unroll not more than two revolutions, replace, and roll up again, repeat until the spring regains proper tension. If spring is too loose and shade won't roll up, pull shade about halfway down, remove from brackets and roll not more than two revolutions onto the roller before replacing it, and repeat the process if necessary.

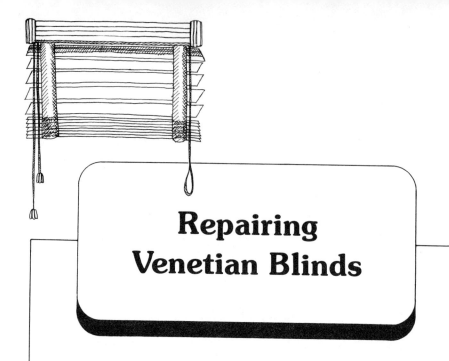

Repairing
Venetian Blinds

Nothing makes a window more unsightly than a damaged venetian blind, one in which slats are broken or hang askew because of a torn tape or broken cord. Repairs are not as complicated as they might seem. Broken slats can easily be replaced. Other problems are usually caused by lift tapes and horizontal ladder tapes that have become torn or by cords that are badly frayed. It's not hard to replace these—and to replace any bent or broken slats in the process. New cords, tapes and plastic pulls are available in a complete package at most hardware stores.

First, open and fully lower the blind; then open the brackets at either end of the head, or top channel, and lift the blind away from the window. Spread it out on the floor or other large working surface. Look it over closely before taking it apart, so you'll know how to get it back together again.

The lift tapes at each side consist of two vertical strips joined by a series of horizontal strips; it is these latter strips that support the slats. The top of each tape is attached to the tilt mechanism and the other end of the tape to the bottom bar, by clamps on metal blinds, staples on wood blinds.

The cord that raises and lowers the blind is one continuous loop. It is first attached to the bottom left corner of the blind, then threaded up between the tapes, across the upper rail and down through the lift-cord lock that is on the right side. The cord then curves back up through the cord-lock mechanism, down through the right-hand tape and is fastened to the bottom bar at the right side. A knot at each end keeps the cord from pulling through the bottom bar. A small clip on the lift cord allows adjustment of the cords so the blind can be pulled up evenly from both sides.

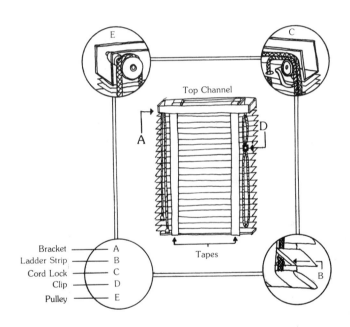

To take the blind apart, first remove the lift cords. The knots holding them in place on the bottom bar are usually concealed by the tapes. Pry the tapes free, untie the knots and pull the cord out from the top. Remove the slats next, by sliding them out from between the tapes. Clean, wash, repaint or replace slats as needed.

To clean slats, use a cream cleaning wax that removes soil and provides a protective finish to make future dusting easier. Using a mitt, you can clean both sides of the slats at the same time; make your own mitt with thumb and forefinger from a soft cloth.

Now the tapes can be removed from the mechanism at the top. This is a good time to dust the inside of the head channel, and to lubricate the lock mechanism with a few squirts of silicone spray lubricant. Lay the new tapes beside the old ones, and cut to the same length. Attach the new tapes to the tilt bar at either side with staples or clamps, as required.

Replace the slats by fitting them between the tapes, resting each on the ladder strips at both sides. When installing the new lift cord, start at the bottom left and thread it up through the hole in each slat; the cord should pass ladder strips on alternate sides. Run the cord across the top and down through the lift-cord lock; thread it through the equalizing clip, then back up through this clip again and then through the cord-lock mechanism. Thread the cord down through the holes of the slats on the right side, again passing ladder strips on alternate sides. Tie knots in the ends of the cord at each side. Staple or clamp the lift-tape ends to the underside of the bottom bar to cover the knots and make a smooth finish.

To replace the tilt cord on the left of the blind, lift it off its pulley, and cut off one plastic pull so that you can slide cord out. Place the new cord over the pulley, and slip new plastic pulls over the ends. Tie a knot in the end of each cord to hold the pulls in place. The blind is now ready for rehanging.

Now that you've tackled one blind, you should be an expert at repairing any others around the house that need it.

Keeping
On The Grass

Do you ever have the urge to pave over your yard and paint it green? Certainly the frustrations of maintaining healthy grass are many, but with some knowledge of lawn-care fundamentals, good planning, proper maintenance, recognition of grass problems and proper use of equipment, you can have a lovely lawn without damaging either health or sanity.

Most lawns get by with some weed control, regular mowing and watering. Fertilizer is precious and is needed to help feed people, not grass. With sensible maintenance, your lawn probably doesn't even need it—after all, it doesn't have to look like a golf course!

Mowing

The object of mowing is to keep the lawn neat without cutting away too much; brown stubble shouldn't show when grass is cut. Don't cut too close; a low-clipped lawn can look shaggy because weeds will show, and you will also increase weed problems—the less grass, the more weeds. It's also a mistake to let grass get too tall before cutting—this shocks the lawn and disrupts its growth.

Keep the mower sharp, and cut when lawn is dry. There is much debate about whether clippings should be left on the ground or removed. Clippings left to decay return some fertility to the soil, but if you feel they're unsightly or will encourage disease, by all means collect them; the fertility lost can be replaced by a single feeding.

A variety of mowers is available—reel, rotary, riders and tractors. Though hand reel mowers are still used, especially for very small plots of grass, power mowers have pretty much taken over. The blades of a rotary mower are less expensive and less likely to need adjustment, and will give you an even cut each time. The rotary is a good maneuverable mower for trimming edges or hard-to-reach areas around obstacles, and it cuts through heavy weeds quite easily. Because of its broad base and floating suspension it works well on rough ground. If you insist on having a putting-green look, then the reel mower is a good choice. The extra time invested in adjustment and maintenance is rewarded by the fine, scissor-like cut and manicured appearance. A reel mower is also good for steep slopes or terraced lawns but not as effective on rough terrain.

If you want to remove clippings, you'll need a bagging attachment. Ease of starting is especially important when using a bagger, as the engine must be stopped each time the bag is emptied. To eliminate laborious starter-rope pulling, gasoline mowers now come with electric-key starting. And of course there are fully electric power mowers; they don't have to be filled with fuel, the noise level is reduced and you simply plug in and go. These are especially good for relatively small lawns but you do have to be careful not to run over the cord, and they can be dangerous to use in wet weather. Rider mowers aren't really necessary unless your lawn is a half acre or more. They do make the mowing job easier, of course, and many have attachments for seeding, fertilizing or removing debris; some even have a snow-removal attachment. The horsepower of a rider is less than that of a tractor, as is the price. Tractors are mainly for very large areas, and of course they have a variety of other uses.

Here are a few other points to keep in mind before purchasing a mower: Consider where the controls are located; on a walk mower they should be on the handle; on a rider they should be directly in front of you. A walk mower should be light enough to turn easily and quickly; front-wheel drive on a power-driven mower increases its handling ability. The cutting-height controls should be easy to reach and safe to operate. Be sure there is a qualified maintenance facility nearby.

Power-mower safety tips:

• Read the instruction manual carefully and follow directions exactly.

• Never refuel a hot or running engine. Refuel outdoors, and don't smoke. Leave room in the fuel tank for gas to expand from sun's heat.

• Before mowing, clear the area of sticks, rocks, wires and other debris.

• Start the mower on level ground.

• Disengage clutches and put the mower in neutral before starting.

• Don't allow children to operate power mowers; keep children and pets away from mowing area.

• Stop engine and disconnect sparkplug wire before doing any repairs.

• Don't use electric mowers on wet grass. The cord should be in good condition at all times and have a ground wire.

• Don't leave running mower unattended.

• Push, don't pull your mower.

• With a conventional power mower, mow slopes sideways; with a riding mower, vertically.

• Stop engine before pushing or riding mower across walks, drives or roads.

• Don't wear loose clothing that could get tangled in moving parts; no shorts, sandals or bare feet. Safety glasses or goggles are also recommended to prevent eye damage from flying objects.

• A power mower with gasoline in the tank shouldn't be stored inside a building where fumes may reach an open flame or spark.

• Allow the engine to cool before storing the machine inside.

A comprehensive safety standard for power mowers has been developed by the Outdoor Power Equipment Institute. Look for the OPEI triangular safety seal when you buy.

Weeds

Weeds may not be as alarming as they seem. Some weeds disappear as grass crowds them out or with regular mowing. Others are controlled with weed killers. Usually they are most susceptible to chemical control when vigorously growing, such as in warm, wet weather. In northern states spring is the time to attack most broad-leafed weeds (chickweed, dandelion, clover, carpetweed, and so forth) while the autumn is right for those whose growth cycle is renewed in the fall. Something is almost always sprouting in the south so weed treatment is useful anytime. A weed killer, or herbicide, shouldn't be applied during very hot days or summer drought; the latter could toughen weeds and cause them to become less susceptible to chemicals. Some weed killers are absorbed through the leaves and the weed dies slowly as it twists and curls; with both the roots and tops affected there is seldom any resprouting. Sometimes granular weed killers don't stick well to foliage; in this case spread them when leaves are moist with dew. Sprays usually stick better than dry materials, but will stick even better if a pinch of detergent is added to the solution. Weed killers should be used exactly as directed: Using too little won't kill the weeds; too much can damage the grass and soil. Some products vaporize and the vapors can injure or kill garden plants; ask for low-volatile types when purchasing.

Of the annual grassy weeds, crabgrass is the most annoying. It starts from seed each spring and sprouts when soil warms to about 60 degrees; with hot weather and lots of rain the plant expands rapidly. From middle to late summer it produces wiry crowfoot-shape seed heads; just before frost the plant turns an unattractive yellow. It doesn't do much good to try to remove the dead plants since this scatters the seed, sowing it for the next year. It's better to use a pre-emergence or preventer chemical in the spring when the crabgrass seedlings sprout. These chemicals include Dacthal, or arsonates such as Bandane, Chlordane, Betasan and Tupersan. Good preventers are effective for months. Because good preventers also destroy newly sown lawn seed they should be used only on established lawns. Even if you're going to overseed a sparse lawn, do it well ahead of applying a crabgrass preventer, or wait until fall. Follow the product's instructions for uniform spreading over the lawn—granular preventers can be dropped from a mechanical spreader. Don't bother putting crabgrass preventer in shaded areas; crabgrass doesn't grow in the shade.

If you've missed killing grassy weeds as they sprout, there are chemical sprays that you can use later. Usually two applications, about a week apart, are needed.

Watering

Watering is seldom essential in climates where rainfall is at least 25 inches per year, but in really arid areas a good lawn is impossible without it. If you need to water because of a dry period, one inch per week should be enough.

Rather than frequent light watering, it is better to provide one good soaking each week to make sure that the ground is deeply penetrated. Daily watering only brings the roots to the surface, searching for the extra moisture, and exposes them to heat. It also encourages weeds. If you have a good rain, forget about watering that week. Watering at night is not advisable as fungus can grow overnight; watering in the morning allows the lawn to dry during the day.

Sprinklers are of various types—pulsating, revolving, oscillating; some shut off when a preselected amount of water is used. If your water pressure is not very good, a simple, perforated, non-moving type is best. With excellent water pressure, an oscillating, revolving or automatic sprinkler will cover a larger area.

Rubber hoses are heavy to handle and can be damaged by the sun; however, they resist kinking and have good flexibility. *Plastic hoses* are lightweight, less expensive and take up less storage space. Don't buy any hose smaller than one-half inch in size.

Tools

Grass shears and *edge trimmers* are very convenient for trimming along flower beds, fences and pavement, where the mower misses. Some grass shears have Teflon-coated blades for smooth cutting and easier cleaning; some have long handles to save a lot of stooping. Also, there are cordless electric shears that trim an average-size suburban lot on one charge and save a lot of wear and tear on your hands.

Handy *small tools* sometimes needed in caring for a lawn

include a long-handled dandelion knife, crabgrass root gripper and lifter, long-handled weeder, small weeding hoe. You'll want to have a weed-killer applicator of some kind, and you can choose from an array that spray, squirt, sprinkle, douse or dust with the pull of a trigger or twist of a valve. Once these applicators are used for weed killing they should not be used for anything else.

Other Problems

Special lawn problems that might occur are insects, disease, yellowish grass. A uniformly spread insecticide is the usual cure for insects. However, some build up a resistance to one insecticide and you may have to switch brands occasionally. You can also help check lawn disease by applying a fungicide before the trouble appears. In the North a preventive treatment for snow mold should be done in late autumn. Since disease thrives mostly in humid conditions, watering should be halted for a while if disease is detected. Yellowish grass can be caused by a lack of nitrogen or a disease requiring a fungicide. If you find small patches of dead grass, you can either reseed or replace with new sod. You can buy as little as one or two yards of sod for about 40 to 50 cents a yard.

Reviving Your Rusty Rakes and Other Garden Tools

Fall is the time to clean and store the garden tools that have been getting such heavy use the past few months. If you aren't already doing so, keep these everyday care tips in mind for next season.

Metal garden tools such as hoes, rakes and shovels are susceptible to rusting, so after each use wipe off clinging soil with paper towels or old rags. Dried-on soil can be removed by scraping with a wire brush or abrasive cloth. Ideally, the tools should then be wiped with an oily rag (lubricating oil). To be safe, store the oily rag in a covered container. You may find it more convenient to keep a bucket filled with garden or builders' sand mixed with lubricating oil, so the tools can be dipped in for a quick cleaning and oiling. If a handle breaks, it doesn't always mean the tool has to be discarded. Replacement handles for better tools are usually available in garden supply and hardware stores: just bring the tool with you to make sure you get the correct size and type.

To store hand tools for the season, clean them as described above and remove any rust by rubbing with steel wool or using a rust remover. Now is the time to sharpen tools that need it in order to avoid delays in the spring. To sharpen the tools yourself secure the shank of the tool in a vise, with the cutting edge facing up. Using a flat single-cut file, sharpen the top cutting edge of the tool, filing only on the down stroke and into the blade. This technique prevents burrs or unevenness on the cutting edge. Scissors and clippers should be sharpened from the bevel side only, with the file traveling from the heel to the point of the blade at each stroke. Whether tools are sharpened or not, wipe the metal surface of the tool with lubricating oil before storing. If wooden handles are rough or splintered, smooth them with light sandpaper and then rub boiled linseed oil into the handle as a preservative. Wipe the excess oil away with another cloth.

Sprayers should be flushed of any residue and allowed to air dry thoroughly. Examine the nozzle for clogging or grit and remove with a piece of thin wire. Examine washers and replace them if worn. Tools with moving parts, such as shears, pruners and trimmers, should be lubricated. Some electric garden tools require a dry spray lubricant (silicone) rather than an oily one; find out what the manufacturer recommends. Hoses should be completely drained of water and wiped clean on the outside. Rinse out watering cans and make sure metal ones are dried to prevent rusting.

All garden tools should be kept in a weather-protected area (preferably indoors) where it is cool and dry. Hanging larger tools from the wall is a safe way to store them. You can purchase ready-made tool holder/organizers which mount on the wall. Or you can drill a hole in the end of a wooden handled tool and hang from a nail. On concrete walls, use masonry nails. Another method is to attach a screw eye to the top of the handle and hang the tool from hooks or pegs. Store hoses on a reel or coil and hang so that the hose is not pressed out of shape. Tools that aren't suitable for hanging can be wrapped in plastic bags and stored on shelves or in boxes.

This is a good time to mark your tools so they are identifiable as your property. Brightly colored tools are also easier to see when on the ground, so you don't accidentally step on them. Spray paint the tool handles, or wrap them with colorful waterproof tape.

The care of power equipment, particularly lawn mowers, is a bit more involved, so always refer to your owner's manual for specific advice. As a general guideline, drain all the gasoline from gas powered mowers, and remove the battery from battery powered mowers. Store the battery indoors in a warm, dry place. Check the line cord of an electric mower for any breaks or fraying and have it repaired. Clean grass clippings from the blades and bottom of the mower and oil the parts according to manufacturer's directions. If the blades need sharpening, have this done professionally. Before storing, cover the mower with a large plastic sheet to protect it from dust and moisture.

Patching Up
the Driveway

The effect of weather, plus general wear and age, will cause driveways to develop cracks, holes and broken sections. For this repair job you'll need some help; as the bags of patching compound are very heavy, perhaps you could make it a week-end project for the whole family.

Since blacktop (asphalt) driveways are the most common, we will concentrate on them. Concrete driveways can also be repaired with asphalt compounds; however, concrete compounds cannot be used on asphalt. Asphalt patching comes in heavy paper bags and has fine gravel already added to the asphalt binder, ready for use; you can usually get it at hardware stores or lumber yards. This material is easiest to work with in warm weather so if the weather is below 60 degrees, it's a good idea to keep it indoors overnight.

Begin by removing leaves, loose crumbling material, dirt or other debris from the hole being patched. If it's really a deep cavity, more than three inches, say, fill it first with small stones or gravel. Then tamp these down with a heavy piece of wood to make a solid foundation. Shovel asphalt mix into the hole to within about an inch of the top. With the shovel, poke and slice the compound to cut up the lumps and eliminate air pockets. Then tamp the material against the bottom and sides of the hole and pack down very tightly. Now add more asphalt compound to bring the level up to about one-half inch above the surrounding surface. Tamp this down again. Then run one wheel of your automobile back and forth over the patched area until it is both hard and level. A small amount of compound will stick to the tire; if you want to prevent this, lay a piece of plastic sheeting over the patch. Or, use a lawn roller.

Small cracks need only a fine sand mixed with an asphalt sealer; this makes a mud-like mixture which can be troweled over the crack to fill it in. Or use Elmer's Blacktop Crack Sealer which can be quickly applied with a caulking gun. All patches should be left overnight before finishing the job with a sealer.

Special blacktop sealers are sold in hardware stores, paint stores, and building supply centers. They usually come in 5-gallon cans which cover approximately 200 square feet. The sealer material is similar to asphalt patching compound, but contains additives to thin it and make it spreadable. You'll need a large pushbroom or similar brush for this. Again, it's easier to work with the sealer material in warm weather.

Before applying the sealer, sweep the driveway clear of all debris and scrub any oil or grease stains with a heavy-duty cleaner. Then rinse thoroughly with a garden hose and allow to dry. Pour on a puddle of sealer, work in parallel directions, and spread it evenly and smoothly with the pushbroom. You should wet the blacktop thoroughly while keeping the coat quite thin, but not too thin as this will decrease its effectiveness. The sealer label directions usually suggest a recommended coverage of 50 to 100 square feet per gallon. When the complete driveway is covered, rope off the area to keep cars and bicycles away until it is dry. It could dry in about four hours, but it's best to leave it overnight before driving a car on it.

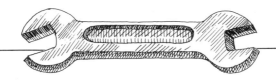

Bicycle Repairs

Major bicycle repairs should be done by a skilled mechanic, but there are many things you can do to keep your bicycle running better, longer and more safely. First, as bicycles vary in design and parts, read your instruction booklet carefully before doing anything. Then you'll be ready to take on some simple parts replacement and repairs. Before doing anything, tighten the handlebars and keep stem well down in fork. If handle grips are worn, replace. Tighten nuts of the seat and keep them tight at all times.

Wheels and Tires

Spin the wheels to see if they are true. If not, check the spokes for tightness and, if necessary, adjust with a spoke wrench, which is inexpensive and is available at any bike store. Tight spokes give off a clear ping when plucked; loose spokes make a much duller sound. Replace broken or bent spokes. Remove the tires and make sure there aren't any spoke heads protruding from the inside of the rim; if there are, file the spokes flush with the spoke nipples so the spokes won't puncture the tube. Move the wheel sideways to see if there is play; if there is, the hub cones need to be tightened. If a wheel runs against the fender, this could mean it's bent or out of line; straightening can be accomplished with a spoke wrench. In order to align, loosen hub nuts and retighten when the wheel is in straight.

Tires should be kept at the proper pressure; this is usually indicated in raised letters on the sidewalls. You can use a hand pump and pressure gauge, or simply use the air pump at your local gas station. Inspect the tires for embedded metal, glass or cinders and remove them carefully.

To change a flat tire: Turn the bike over, resting it on the seat and handlebars. Remove nuts and washers from the axle. Take off the fender braces. The front wheel should come out easily when the axle nuts are loosened. If it's the rear wheel, look for the brake arm (a metal bar about $2\frac{1}{2}$ inches long usually clamped to the frame). Derailleur bikes (five- or ten-speed bikes with a device that switches the chain from one sprocket to another) don't have this arm but will have shift linkage to disconnect. Remove the clamp, push the wheel forward, remove chain from sprocket and lift off wheel. Remove the tire from the wheel with a spoon handle (if you don't have a tire iron) by slipping the tool under the rubber and running it around the rim to get one bead of the tire over it. Pull out inner tube and remove tire. If cord shows in the rubber or there are splits, get a new tire. If there are worn spots in the tube, get a new one; they're inexpensive and patches can cause problems.

To put on new tire, work one edge over the rim of the wheel. Then push the tube under the tire, making sure that the valve stem goes through the hole in the rim. Work other edge over the rim, using the spoon handle to get the last part on, if necessary; sometimes a little talcum powder makes this easier. Carefully fill the tires with air, making sure the tire stays on the rim. When tires are filled to correct pressure, wheel can be replaced. With the front tire, put on the inner nuts that hold the bearings just tight enough so the wheel spins freely; center the tire so it doesn't rub against the front forks or fender; then tighten. With the back wheel, put the chain on the sprocket or sprockets and replace the brake-arm clamp. Tighten the wheel, making certain that it is well centered.

Chain

Clean with a brush and lubricate, but don't oil excessively; this collects dust and causes wear. An occasional drop of oil on each end of all the pins will keep chain operating easily. Most chains are taken apart for cleaning by removing the snap link. Soak the chain in kerosene for half a day or more, sloshing the kerosene over, under and around the chain to remove all soil. Wipe it dry, then bathe it again in light machine oil, working each joint until it moves freely. Dry again and replace on bicycle, adjusting the rear wheel so the chain is neither too loose nor too tight. If chain breaks, remove the broken link and snap on a new master link.

Brakes

With hand brakes there is normally an adjuster nut on the fitting where the cable ends. Adjust this fitting until firm pressure is applied to the rim. Frayed cables and worn brake blocks should be replaced for your own safety. With an uneven coaster brake, it's best to have a serviceman adjust this.

Pedals

Replace worn pedal treads. If the pedal hits the kick stand, the stand may need to be tightened. If the spring on the stand is weak, a new stand should be purchased (they're not expensive). Be sure the pedal axle is tight in the cranks. If bearings are bad or shafts bent, buy new pedals. Get the reflector type for safe driving at night.

Is Your Home Ready For Winter?

At the first cold snap, it's natural to wonder if the furnace is working properly. Wise homeowners who scheduled a complete professional checkup of their heating system during the summer can flip the switch with confidence. For those who didn't, however, there still may be time to see that everything is in working order.

A heating system functions best and most economically when the house is as airtight as possible: properly insulated, weather-stripped, and equipped with storm windows and doors. Ideally you should have six inches of insulation over the top-floor ceiling. It results in considerable fuel savings and will help reduce air-conditioning costs in the summer. Sidewall insulation is desirable, too, though it is best done when the house is being built. Check and seal off those places where air may be entering: Caulk the frames of windows and doors; use weather stripping at movable joints; add door sweeps to loose-fitting doors; stuff large cracks with insulating material and seal them with a caulking compound, smaller cracks with ready-made rope putty. Storm windows and doors that fit tightly and are in good repair will cut in half needlessly lost heat. Though an expensive investment, storm windows will pay for themselves in ten years.

We tend to take the heating system for granted. But there are several necessary adjustments and maintenance jobs for which the homeowner is responsible. Probably the most familiar part of the system is the thermostat. Remove its cover occasionally and gently blow out the accumulated dust and dirt. After about ten years, the thermostat may need to be replaced or at least professionally cleaned and adjusted to assure its sensitivity. The commonest way to waste fuel is to switch the thermostat up and down. On a really cold day, find the temperature setting that is the most comfortable and leave it there. Recommended settings are 70 degrees during the day, 65 degrees during the night and for away-from-home periods of 12 hours or longer. Every degree above 70 degrees increases fuel consumption as much as 3 percent per degree.

Be certain that radiators, grilles, vents and registers in every room are not obstructed by any furnishings. Another source of heat loss is the dust and lint that collects on radiator fins or on convectors and baseboard units. Vacuum them at least once a year. Be sure your radiators are heating all the way across. If one of them isn't, open the vent at the top with a screwdriver or special key provided and let the accumulated air escape until the water flows, at which point you immediately shut the vent.

A clean furnace will provide more heat more economically. Clogged filters hinder air flow and cause the furnace to run excessively. The filters of warm-air furnaces should be inspected monthly and changed from two to three times a winter (some systems have washable filters). It's generally a good idea to keep extra filters on hand. Unless you have a service contract, oil those moving parts that require it by following the instruction manual. Clean scale and rust from the combustion chamber of a hot-water system, and oil the circulator pump. A steam system, found mostly in older houses, may need cleaning if the water in the boiler gauge is surging or agitating. Check the water level at least once a month, and replenish the water if indicated in the sight glass.

If there isn't enough humidity in the air during the winter months, children may develop colds more frequently, furniture dries out and is likely to crack or come unglued, too much annoying static electricity is created, and your fuel bill may become alarmingly high. By keeping the relative humidity at about 40 to 50 percent, people feel more comfortable at a lower temperature. To measure the exact humidity level in your home, a hygrometer or a humidity indicator, which gives the temperature as well, can be purchased for about $8 or $10. If you find it necessary to increase the humidity level, it's relatively easy to add a humidifier to almost any furnace. If the furnace is already equipped with one, and you sense it is not doing its job, the reservoir may need cleaning, float valves should be checked and the plates and pads may need cleaning or replacing. Do this at least twice a year, following the manufacturer's instructions. In hard-water areas such attention should be given more frequently.

A portable, or console, humidifier is the answer if your heating system cannot adapt to a permanent installation. These humidifiers, which look like a piece of living-room furniture, will do an effective job of humidifying the average-size house if placed in a central location and if all inside doors are left open. They range in price from about $50 to $150. To help you when you buy, humidifiers are capacity-rated for water output by the Association of Home Appliance Manufacturers. Look for the AHAM seal. There is a level—60 percent and over—beyond which added moisture may be a liability, causing furniture glue to loosen and frost to form under roof beams. Excess moisture on windows and walls in winter is the clue if you don't have a humidity indicator, and adjustments should be made accordingly.

Electronic or electrostatic air cleaners filter out airborne dust, dirt, pollen, smoke and odors. In addition to contributing to family health and comfort, they help cut down household maintenance costs by preventing dust, soot and grease from settling on walls, furniture and curtains. These benefits come at low cost and with very little extra fuel consumption—not more than the equivalent of a 100-watt bulb. Electronic air cleaners may be added to central forced-air heating and cooling systems for about $300 plus installation. More recently, portable room-size electronic air cleaners, which will do the same job in smaller areas such as apartments and mobile homes, have appeared. Prices start at about $100.

Fundamentally, an air cleaner consists of three filters that function in the following ways: first, a mechanical filter, which traps large particles such as dust, dirt, lint and hair; second, an electronic cell, which places a positive electrical charge on such microscopic particles as smoke and pollen and attracts them onto negative plates where they are held until the plates are washed; and third, a charcoal filter, which absorbs household odors and vapors and breaks down or consumes much of the ozone produced by the strong electric field.

Maintenance, though simple, is important for these devices to perform effectively. Under normal use, every month or two (or according to manufacturer's recommendations), vacuum or wash the mechanical prefilter. Remove the electronic cells and soak in hot detergent solution for about an hour and a half. Follow with a ten-minute soak in clear water. (Some units can be washed in place: Consult the instruction book.) The charcoal filter cannot be cleaned, and must be replaced about once a year. Don't expect dramatic improvement the minute you acquire an air cleaner; its benefits take a while to be felt and will persist with proper maintenance and if only a minimum of outside doors and windows are left open.

In addition, these simple hints will contribute toward getting full value for each fuel dollar spent:

1. If you have a fireplace, be sure the damper is closed when there's no fire going. And while you're enjoying the warm glow of a fire, remember that about 80 percent of its heat goes up the

chimney along with a vast amount of the warm air you have paid to heat.

2. Sunshine is free energy: In the daytime, open wide all curtains, shades and blinds on the sunny side of the house to make maximum use of the sun's warmth; at night, close them to keep the heat from escaping.

3. Keep the opening and closing of outside doors at a minimum. Warm air pours out each time a door is opened, forcing the furnace to work harder. Train your children, too, to see that doors are always tightly closed.

4. Shut off unused rooms; turn off the heat and keep the doors closed. Consider weather stripping round each door to be sure it's tightly sealed.

5. Try living with the thermostat set one or two degrees lower than usual. You may discover you don't need as much heat as you thought.

If the furnace stops some cold winter night, check the following possibilities before calling a serviceman.

1. *Thermostat:* It may have been turned down without your knowing it.

2. *Fuses:* Check them all—the main fuse, the one controlling the burner and the master switch.

3. *Filters* on a forced-air system: They may simply need to be cleaned—the burner is working but the house remains cool.

4. *Fuel:* Oil may have run out; a steam system may need water (the furnace will stop if there's not enough water); pilot light may have gone out on a gas furnace—relight it, following manufacturer's instructions on burner.

If none of these solutions work, call a serviceman.

How To Save on Winter Fuel Bills

If your house is adequately insulated, you can realize substantial savings in fuel costs. In fact, a well-buttoned-up house could cut the bill in half. For example: Just three inches of insulation in the ceilings of top-floor rooms can reduce fuel consumption by 34 percent; two inches under crawl-space floors can save 15 percent; two inches in the walls saves 10 percent. And if you install four inches of ceiling and three inches of wall insulation, fuel needs can be slimmed by 47 percent; add an additional three inches in the ceiling (the most important place for insulation) and you cut total fuel requirements to half those of an uninsulated house. Storm windows and doors can save another 10 percent; caulking cracks and weather-stripping doors and windows can also help. In addition to preventing indoor heat from escaping in winter, insulation helps to keep summer heat from seeping inside; it saves you money all year.

Despite the savings that could be realized, two-thirds of American houses are insufficiently or improperly insulated, and some have no insulation at all. Energy experts say that if these houses had at least six inches of insulation in their attics, everyone could be more comfortable for less money. And while home-insulation costs vary with the kind of materials used, size of the house and geographical location, the average cost of adding this six inches is quite reasonable—within the $100 to $200 range.

Insulation Materials

The effectiveness of insulation materials is specified by an R factor, which stands for "resistance to heat flow." When buying insulation look for the letter R plus a number; the higher the R value the better. For example, R-19 is considered excellent for ceilings. There are four basic types:

Blankets and batts, made of fiber glass or mineral wool with asphalt-paper or foil vapor barriers, have the insulating material enclosed in a continuous envelope. Flanges on the sides of both permit them to be stapled to a frame. Blankets and batts are similar in appearance but are sold in different forms. Blankets come in rolls of 40 to 100 feet in length and 15 or 23 inches wide to fit between standard 16- and 24-inch stud-joist-rafter spacings. Batts are usually in four- or eight-foot lengths by 15- or 23-inch widths for easy handling and for use in tight spots.

Loose-fill insulation—fibrous or granular—is sold in bulk, each bag containing about 3 cubic feet, and is usually poured or blown into wall and floor spaces that are formed by studs and joists. Since little processing and packaging is used, it is low in cost. Because it is blown into walls with a special blower, this type is often used in old houses where there is no insulation behind the walls. This type of material works well but doesn't provide a vapor barrier (polyethylene plastic sheeting can be installed in addition for this purpose) and it does settle over a period of years.

Insulation board of wood fiber comes in sheets, panels, planks and tiles; it can be cut and fitted with regular tools, and can be used by itself as an actual wall in new construction, or placed right over old walls. With the combination of structural strength and insulating properties, it is especially good for ceilings.

Reflective insulation has become quite popular. Made from

reflective foils such as aluminum or polished metallic flakes that adhere to reinforced paper, it provides a shiny, mirrorlike surface that bounces radiant heat back from where it came. It is available with or without an attached insulation batt, but without the batt it must be placed so there is dead air space on both sides.

Although once a house is constructed it might be difficult to do a thorough insulation job, it can be done. If it isn't economically feasible to insulate the walls, the top-floor ceiling, at least, should be done. Loose-fill insulation can be poured between floor joists in an unheated attic, or a professional can blow insulation into the walls and attic floors. Floors above unheated crawl spaces can be insulated with blankets, batts or insulation board; staple blankets and batts between floor joists with the vapor barrier side up. Insulation board can be cut slightly wider than the space between the joists and pressed in by hand.

When a profesional insulation contractor is needed, you can find one by asking your local utility company for suggestions, consulting friends and neighbors, or looking in the Yellow Pages of your phone directory under "Insulation Contractors—Cold & Heat." Check his reputation and work.

Weather Stripping and Caulking

The goal of home insulation is to form a thermal blanket around the house; caulking and weather stripping help to fill the inevitable gaps. Having a front door that is not weather-stripped is similar to having a six-inch hole in the exterior wall of your house. Install weather stripping around the windows as well. Doors that lead to basements, attics and garages should be sealed tightly with weather stripping when not in use or if the rooms aren't heated. You should caulk cracks and any other openings around windows, doors and wherever there is a joint in the siding of the house in order to seal off air seepage everywhere. Caulking compound is available in bulk form in a can or in cartridges.

Storm Windows and Doors

Poorly constructed windows can negate much of a house's insulation, with a resultant heat loss of up to 40 percent. Top-quality wood windows with double-pane insulating glass or aluminum storm windows can reduce this loss measurably. Wood is one of nature's best insulators and with double-pane insulating glass there is no need for storm windows. Conducted heat loss through double-pane glass can be cut by as much as 35 percent, compared to single-glazed units without storm windows. With factory-applied weather stripping these windows are heat-tight.

Combination storm-and-screen windows have three tracks—two for sliding panes of glass and one for a screen. With these, the seasonal change-around has been simplified; everything is operated from inside. Windows and screens should have good interlocks between panels to seal out weather and insects. Screens should be on the inside track to protect them against winter weather. Combination units have three basic finishes: mill, anodized aluminum or baked enamel. Mill is exposed aluminum just as it comes from the mill; it has a tendency to pit and corrode, especially near seashore areas. Anodized windows offer better corrosion resistance but are still not quite as serviceable as baked enamel. Combination units are available from many manufacturers and cost about $20 and up.

A high-quality storm door could range in price from $50 to over $75, and style has a big effect on price. A good door will have a sturdy protective grill over the bottom glass.

Additional Materials

There are other ways of providing airtight, fuel-saving areas in the home. For example, sheets of clear plastic attached to windows convert wind-swept rooms into draft-free ones. This material, cut with shears, can be easily and quickly tacked or stapled to an average-size window for about $1.50 (or 45 cents per square foot). People who rent may prefer this inexpensive yet effective and durable means of insulating that can bring about a 30 percent saving on fuel.

There is also a metalized transparent plastic film that can be applied to window glass. The purpose of this material is to reduce the sun's heat and eliminate glare without blotting out light. Besides reducing cooling costs in the summer, it works in the opposite fashion in the winter, reflecting fuel-induced heat back into the room. This reflective film is more or less permanent, although it can be peeled off, if desired. The Yellow Pages list dealer-installers under "Glass Coating and Tinting." There are new do-it-yourself versions of the film—thinner, easy-to-handle, adhesive-backed sheets that only need to be moistened with water to stick to windows. The material is available in some department stores and home centers in rolls of various widths, lengths and colors. Additionally, solar shades of clear polyester film serve the same purpose, but function as regular window shades. These can be found in custom shade shops.

Putting Summer in Cold Storage

Here is a guide to readying and storing your family's summer gear for the winter—to give it a longer life and avoid having to make expensive repairs and replacements next spring.

Power Mowers

Remove caked-on dirt and grass clippings with a putty knife or stiff brush. Remove the battery. Drain gasoline from tank, fuel lines and carburetor, and oil from crankcase; refill with fresh oil. Disconnect the spark-plug wire and remove spark plug; pour some oil into opening and manually pull the starter rope to distribute the oil within the cylinder to protect against rust; replace spark plug, but leave wire off to prevent the machine's being accidentally started. Remove the air cleaner and wash in detergent solution or gasoline; add a small amount of oil to the filter and oil cup. Clean and sharpen blades (or have them professionally sharpened). Coat blades with a light film of heavy oil to prevent rust. Check owner's manual for specific instructions on lubrication, tire inflation, and so on. Wrap mower loosely in canvas or plastic to keep out dust and moisture.

Outdoor Furniture

For wrought iron, a coat of rust-inhibiting paint is a good preventive measure, but save a final paint job for spring. Wrap chair and table legs in newspaper. Protect glass tabletops with newspapers, an old blanket or chair cushions.

For wood furniture, repair loose parts, broken wheels, etc., to prevent warping and misalignment. Redwood furniture in good condition can be left outdoors but a covering of some sort is advisable.

Vinyl cushions should be washed with detergent and water. When they are thoroughly dry, cover with plastic and store off the ground in a dry place.

Garden Hose

Drain out all water, and brush threads on each coupling. Coil the hose around a regular hose hanger or reel, join the couplings and store in your garage or shed.

Lawn and Garden Tools

Clean all dirt and rust from metal surfaces with a wire brush, followed by sandpaper or steel wool and, if necessary, a chemical rust remover. When clean and dry, coat with penetrating oil or a rust preventive. Repair wooden handles with waterproof glue. Store small tools in a covered box; hang long-handled tools from garage wall.

Bicycles

If the bike is being stored longer than a month, wipe all metal parts with a cloth saturated in machine oil (SAE 20) to prevent rust and dirt accumulation. Suspend the bike from the seat and the handlebar stem with a rope or bicycle hook; if you let it rest on its tires, they may rot. (Storage in plastic will let moisture accumulate and cause rusting.) In the spring, use mild soapsuds to wipe off the oil, and reinflate the tires to the recommended pressure.

Tennis and Badminton Racquets

Store wooden racquets in a press, and keep both wood *and* metal racquets in canvas covers—in a dry place. (A little talcum powder inside the cover helps absorb moisture.) Used tennis balls probably aren't worth saving; they'll have lost their bounce by spring.

Golf Clubs

Wash the irons in water and detergent—with a brush, if necessary, to remove dirt. Wax the woods with a wood-floor wax or furniture polish. Do not store clubs near heat. Most golf bags are of vinyl and should merely be washed off with soap and water. Clean leather bags with saddle soap. Clean the wheels of the golf cart, oil them and cover the cart to keep it clean and dry.

Inflatable Water Toys, including Boats

Clean with soap and water, deflate and fold. Store in the house, where there is some warmth (cracking can occur in the cold).

Boats

While the boat is still in the water, remove everything removable—clothes, linens, dishes, cushions, etc.—and store in a dry, rodent-free place. Remove mast and boom from a sailboat, and store flat and straight, out of the weather. Wash sails, dry and fold, and store flat, out of the sunlight. Hose down and scrub deck.

Once the boat is out of the water, clean bottom with fresh water to remove barnacles and other marine growth. Drain sinks, showers, toilets, etc., and leave drains open so that any remaining moisture won't freeze. Whether motor is an inboard or outboard, drain the oil and gasoline; then change the oil. Follow manufacturer's directions on the use of antifreeze and to determine whether it will be necessary to remove the engine. Go over the electrical system; remove and charge batteries. Clean all hardware with a good metal cleaner; then wax to prevent pitting and corrosion.

If hull is wooden, varnish appropriate places outside. Throw some salt in the bilge so that any rainwater will turn to salt water (dry rot thrives on fresh water; salt water kills it). Clean, wax and buff the bottom of fiber-glass boats.

Store the boat in a cradle or on a trailer (make certain that rollers are properly adjusted to avoid hull distortion). Wooden boats are best stored outdoors; the moisture in the air prevents drying out and shrinkage. Cover with a tarpaulin or similar covering.

Store fiber-glass and aluminum hulls indoors in unheated area—heat may dry out the paint. If they *must* be left outdoors, protect with a cover.

Boat covers should permit rain and snow to drain off; give ventilation.

Swimming Pools

For aboveground pools, follow manufacturer's directions for draining. If left filled, let out water to recommended level and add algae-control chemicals according to manufacturer's recommendations. Do not use chlorine rings or canisters, as they may bleach the liner. To prevent scuffing of the wall or liner, or ice damage, add logs, air-filled plastic buffers or an old tire, and secure to at least two sides of the pool. Turn off electricity and tape the switch in "off" position, or disconnect at terminal box. Cover pool.

In-ground pools: Leave water in the pool during the off-season, particularly in colder climates; freezing and thawing can cause the walls of an empty pool to buckle. Lower the waterline about a foot to prevent ice forming underneath coping or tile, and drain all water from pipes and filter. For care of pumps, filters, chlorinators, etc., follow manufacturer's directions. Protect exposed equipment (such as filters and skimmers) or, if they are easily removable, store in a dry place. Treat water with an algae-control chemical and, if possible, cover the entire pool.

Recreational Vehicles
(campers, trailers, etc.)

Remove all bedding, clothes and food. Drain all water, no matter whether it is pressurized or pump system, and add an antifreeze as recommended by dealer or owner's manual. Drain toilet; add an antifreeze to the holding tank and to sink traps. The battery should be up to full charge; remove only in very cold climates. Turn gas off at the bottle. Clean and defrost refrigerator and leave door ajar. Unplug all 110V appliances. Repair exterior holes or leaks with caulking to keep out insects and mice. Check roof and, if necessary, coat with a fibrous aluminum paint. Cover air conditioner with a cover that "breathes." Lock vehicle and jack it up to remove weight from tires. If you are unable to store the vehicle yourself, in line with your community's rules for such storage, check the nearest campground, which will probably store it for a fee.

Systems That Warn If Fire's Afoot

Like so many things in nature, fire has two faces to show—one is the benevolent, life-giving force we know so well; the other is a force of destruction that hundreds of thousands of Americans face annually in their own homes! But there is something you can do to protect you and your family from possible danger.

Heat detectors, either mechanical or electric, are the simplest and least expensive fire-protection devices. They are sensitive to the temperature of the area in which they are located, reacting to a high (over 135°F) or an unusually rapid increase in temperature. There are two basic types of mechanical heat detectors. The gas-operated kind contains an element that melts at a pre-set temperature, thereby releasing a form of carbon through a horn and sounding the alarm. The spring-action heat detector has an element which, when exposed to abnormal heat, releases a spring to sound the alarm. Electric heat detectors, however, have a thermostat which senses abnormal heat and signals a control unit to set off the alarm.

Smoke detectors, either electric or battery powered, are somewhat more sophisticated, and there are two main types. The photoelectric detector reacts when its light beam is scattered by smoke particles. The "light" in this case is a special bulb whose beam is synchronized with an electric current in the detector. When smoke obscures the light, the current is reduced and the alarm is triggered. The other type of smoke detector is the ion chamber. This works on basically the same principle as the photoelectric detector, except that instead of a light beam, the air inside the detector itself is electrically charged. When smoke enters, it reduces the flow of electrical current and sets off the alarm.

Heat detectors function well in the event of a rapidly developing hot fire. However, if the fire is slow-burning and smoldering, the alarm in a heat detector might not go off until the smoke has spread and become deadly (and it is smoke and toxic gases that kill most fire victims). Smoke detectors, however, react to the first bit of smoke—minutes before the area becomes hot enough to trigger the heat detector. The National Fire Protection Agency recommends smoke detectors since they react to both rapid-burning and smoldering fires.

The ceiling is the best place to put a heat or smoke detector since both heat and smoke rise before they spread. The ceiling is also an unobstructed area on which to install the system, and such positioning makes maximum use of its coverage (in a large room it is sometimes necessary to have more than one detector—be sure you are fully protected). If you have to put the unit on the wall, make certain nothing is blocking it. It should be mounted not more than 12 inches from the ceiling, and not closer than six inches (the six-inch area between ceiling and wall, especially in the corners, is "dead" air space and heat and smoke are slow to reach it). Since most fatal fires take place between midnight and six AM, the detector should be located between the bedrooms and the rest of the house. If a house has more than one floor, the top of each staircase is the place for the basic detectors. For maximum protection, however, there should be a detector in each room.

What should you look for as you're shopping for a system?

• The alarm should ring for at least four minutes, and should be loud enough to be heard in all bedrooms with the doors shut.

• There should be a "trouble signal," distinct from the alarm, to indicate when batteries run down, photoelectric bulb burns out, etc. And it should be a signal that will continue to warn you for seven days.

• A battery-powered unit should have a heavy-duty type battery that monitors itself and triggers the trouble signal when it is about to run down.

• A spare bulb should be supplied in or on the alarm station if the system is photoelectric, so you will never be left without the proper parts.

• A secondary power supply for an electric system is desirable, so that if your electrical power goes off, your home will not be unprotected.

• Included with the system should be full instructions on installation, operation and maintenance. (Most single-station systems are small, lightweight and easy to install and maintain.) In order to be certain that the detection system is working you should make weekly tests, as well as periodically replace bulbs and batteries.

Heat- and smoke-detection systems range in price from $22 to over $1,000. A mechanical, single-station (which means everything in one unit) heat detector will cost from $22 to $70 and require little installation work. A single-station smoke detector, again with almost no installation problems, will run from $50 to $100. A system with more than one station can run $100 to $150 before installation. More elaborate systems including at least one smoke detector and ten heat detectors can cost from $375 to $1,100, including installation costs. The system you choose will depend on the size of your home, and the location where you plan to install it.

Getting House Pests To Bug Off

When cockroaches, ants, rodents and other pests crawl into your home, you must wish they'd use all those legs to crawl right out again. Sometimes you may feel you're actually having open house for pests, and this is one time you *don't* want to be the hostess with the mostest. Unlike the FBI Ten Most Wanted List, home and apartment dwellers have another list—of the Ten Most UNwanted characters. The list includes the uninvited creeping and crawling pests that descend on your home and which aren't going to leave of their own accord! Let's look at this list and see why its members are a nuisance, damaging, and unhealthy—and what can be done about them.

Cockroaches

Because of their number, cockroaches are Public Enemy Number One. They are persistent pests and regardless of where you live they can get in. They are the greatest problem in multiple dwellings where they may migrate from one apartment to another. But they can also show up in a suburban home by hitching a ride in a bag of groceries. Even if you live on the top floor of a high-rise, you're still not immune from roaches; they have a way of crawling up drain or waterpipes. Even under the most sanitary conditions roaches can arrive from a nearby infestation. Roaches thrive on food but in a pinch they'll also eat wallpaper paste and book bindings. Besides eating, they soil fabrics and carry filth along with germs; have a habit of spitting offensive inklike juices around the home; and have an emotional and psychological effect on most people.

Since they breed at a rapid rate, once roaches get ahead of you you have a real problem. To keep ahead of *them,* observe good housekeeping rules, especially in the kitchen. Roaches *must* have water, the reason you frequently find them around sinks. They eat anything that is soft enough to bite, and show up wherever opened food packages such as cereals, crackers and dog food are available. Keep food packages closed or in tight containers, immediately wipe up food spills and crumbs (they love these).

Roaches are secretive, hiding in cracks, clocks, and behind wall hangings during the day; they come out at night in search of food. Since cleanliness is essential to avoid infestations, clean thoroughly *every* evening, leaving no particles of food on counters or floor, no open containers or unwrapped food on the counter, no dirty dishes in the sink, and no rubbish inside the house. If there's no food around, roaches won't waste their time visiting you and will depart for more rewarding pastures.

Control of small infestations may not be difficult: spraying cracks under cabinets, along baseboards or drainpipe openings with an insecticide containing chlordane, diazinon or pyrethrin may be sufficient. Heavy infestations are a bit more difficult because you must find *all* the hiding places and spray them. This is a problem in cabinets where dishes and food are stored as they must be removed before spraying and the shelves washed before using again. Another solution is to fill the cracks in these cabinets with putty or caulking. For an expert, thorough job, contact a professional pest-control company. They are listed in the Yellow Pages under "pest control" or "exterminators". Look for a firm that advertises its membership in the National Pest Control Association, a good sign that they are reputable.

Grain Beetles

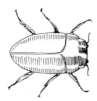

Other kitchen and pantry pests are grain beetles, flour and meal moths. Some are rather specialized in their food choice: bean weevils attack only legumes; rice weevils are partial to whole grains but will also attack macaroni; the confused flour beetle isn't confused about its taste for flour, cereal and other grain products as well as dried fruit; and the sawtooth grain beetle, in addition to flour and cereals, favors spaghetti, macaroni, and nut meats, and has a sweet tooth for cocoa and other chocolate.

Check stored grain products periodically; if there is an infestation the larvae and adults are visible. Throw out the effected product and if any of it has spilled on your counters or in cracks or crevices be sure to wipe it up immediately. Cracks in the cabinets may also be cleaned with a vacuum-cleaner crevice-tool attachment. Thoroughly wash cabinets and counters. Then apply a two-percent solution of chlordane; let dry, and apply new shelf paper. When replacing grain products, buy everything in smaller quantities, and inspect immediately to make sure they're free of pests; then store.

Carpet Beetles

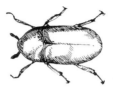

Carpet beetles and clothes moths are not the big problem they once were because of the wide use of synthetics and the fact that most carpets are moth-proofed during manufacturing. But black carpet beetles thrive on lint accumulation in cracks and floorboards and on protein products, especially dry dog food. The furniture carpet beetle is partial to upholstery. The larvae grubs eat holes in fabric to the point where fibers may fall out when fabric is brushed.

Beetles enter your home or apartment in a number of ways: on flowers you've brought from a garden or greenhouse or by hitchhiking on articles containing wool or other animal fibers. If carpet beetles are discovered, vacuum carpeting regularly and thoroughly to get rid of the eggs and grubs, especially under sofas, tables and furniture that are seldom moved or where there is little traffic. Dry-cleaning the rug will destroy any insect life remaining. Also spray an insecticide along the edge of floor and baseboards and on the floor under the edge of rugs.

House Ants

There are many different varieties of these very specialized creatures. Contrary to the belief that they live only in ant hills and depend on picnics for their support, they have a variety of life styles. Some breed outdoors only, others breed indoors; some feed only on other insects, others love grease in almost any form; some are seed eaters; some eat anything man eats, others won't touch human food. Tiny light-yellow varieties may be found nesting in little-used glassware, empty soft-drink bottles, or even in hollow handles of kitchen utensils that have not been used in a while. The brown-colored cornfield ant nests outside but will come into the house to get carelessly left food bits. Yellow ants come through basement cracks only once a year, during winter, when they're swarming. Bits of food on counters and the floor may not matter to humans, but they're gold mines for the ants.

Cleanliness in the kitchen and pantry, especially on the floor next to baseboards and the base of cabinets, helps prevent ant infestation. Once they find attractive food they invade the cabinets. There are baits and mixes to kill ants, but carefully study the labels for preparation and use. Some ant baits are packed in sealed metal containers with directions for making holes in the sides to admit the ants; the method makes them safe for use around children and pets.

Carpenter Ants

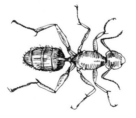

Sometimes confused with termites that actually eat wood, these ants merely tunnel into wood. They form a cavity through a soft spot and discard the wood fragments. The sawdust usually falls to the ground below the nest's entrance. Their favorite nesting spots are associated with moisture, such as wood affected by water seepage from plugged drain gutters, poorly fitted or damaged siding, between the roof and ceiling of flat deck porches, hollow posts and columns, leaking doors and window frames. The workers of this species forage inside for food, while the colony lives outside. Carpenter ants travel singly and don't make trails, so sprays aren't very effective. It's best to spray directly into the nest.

Termites

Extremely destructive, termites do more damage than lightning, tornadoes or arson. About two million of the roughly 50 million dwellings in the U.S. have been attacked by termites. Unfortunately modern man provides this wood-destroying pest with an idyllic environment—warmth, moisture and plenty of food—in boards, timbers and other wooden members of a house. The nicely heated crawlspaces in most buildings and slab construction put termites within easy reach of tasty building timbers.

Termites nest in the ground and get to the wood in buildings through filled masonry porches, cracks in the foundation and so forth. They work only within wood and are seen only when winged adults swarm into the building as early as January and as late as July. They may appear by the hundreds, suddenly emerging from infested wood. Soon after, they break off their wings and run about seeking moist soil. If termites are discovered they can't be controlled by the homeowner. The important thing is don't panic. Termites work slowly so it's best to take the time to select an ethical, trained exterminator. He uses a professional treatment, a long-lasting chemical barrier that is put into the soil circling the home. It cuts termites off as they travel in the soil to the house. To prevent an invasion of termites, have the soil pre-treated as the house is being built. It's effective for twenty years or more and is much less expensive at this time. Another preventative measure—don't stack wood against the house. Before buying a house it's wise to have a termite inspection. In fact, it is sometimes required, such as when getting FHA and VA home loans. In high termite areas—east and west coasts and southern states—it's a good investment to have a termite inspection every one to three years.

Silverfish

These insects prefer warm, damp locations for breeding and travel by night. They're abundant in basements near the furnace and thrive in undisturbed areas such as an attic during the summer. They love starchy items such as paper, paste or sizing, book bindings, piles of discarded newspapers, highly starched linens in storage. You can get rid of silverfish with a household spray containing chlordane, malathion, diazinon, or pyrethrin. If possible, apply sprays to the breeding areas such as the floor, shelving, and under cartons and other stored material. One application may not be enough; if needed, spray at two-week intervals.

Rats

Though found mostly in industrial and slum areas, rats are also attracted to suburban homes if they're located next to a stream, have birdfeed around, an apple tree or an outdoor dog. They feed on a dog's food and drink, as well as birdfeed and apples. In disadvantaged areas poor sanitation, careless handling of garbage and improperly protected buildings give rats nearly perfect living and breeding conditions. But even in suburbia, rats thrive on a rich food supply in sewers as the result of food-waste disposers. Make sure there are no open basement windows, or uncapped sewer pipes.

Mice

House mice are not as meek as some may think; in fact, they're very shrewd. They steal food to appease their insatiable appetite, pursue food under the most impossible circumstances, can get through a very tiny opening, and with enough food can set up a housekeeping establishment which is soon several generations in size. You'll notice them in the fall when they come in from the outdoors through unscreened windows and holes around pipes. Even the tiniest spaces should be sealed and all common entrance points plugged. They're also very quiet, you hardly know they're around (until, to your horror, they come out of their hiding place).

Mouse traps are still the most effective way to control mice. Contrary to popular belief, cheese is not the best bait; mice love peanut butter, cooked bacon, gumdrops, and cotton which they use for their nests. But because mice don't travel far, trap placement is important; you may have to move it around a bit until you get close enough.

Fleas and Ticks

Fleas are increasingly annoying because of the abundance of dogs and cats and the close proximity in which we live. Adult fleas live in the hairs of their host and pierce the skin to suck blood for feed. Eggs are deposited among the hairs and are usually shaken off. Large numbers of eggs can accumulate where the animals sleep. To reduce large infestations destroy or spray animal bedding and spray the floors of all rooms used by the pet. Control the fleas on the pet by using a product whose label specifies the type of pet on which it is to be used.

A dog freely running through grass and brush can pick up hundreds of ticks which quickly multiply and infest a variety of hiding places in the home. Some occur only in small numbers when they leave the dog. Some develop from eggs in cracks and under rugs. This kind of infestation develops, however, only when a dog has been infested for some time. Some adult ticks may attack people and are capable of transmitting spotted fever. A spray for ticks may be applied to the baseboards, under furniture, and around edges of rugs.

Pest Control

The key to the control of pests lies in the proper use of pesticides.

• Before purchasing a pesticide, carefully check the label to be sure it lists the name of the problem pest. Pesticides must be registered with the Environmental Protection Agency and must be safe in order to be registered. The label will indicate an EPA registration number, and if none is there beware.

• Read the label carefully *each time* you use the product. Also read leaflets of instructions if included.

• Follow directions exactly.

• Be careful not to get pesticides on food, dishes or cooking utensils.

• Remove pets, their water and food pans before applying pesticides.

• Avoid breathing pesticidal dusts or mists when the label warns against it. Keep face away from the cap when opening.

• If using poison bait, place out of reach of children and pets.

• Avoid contact of any pesticide with the skin.

• Don't smoke while handling pesticides.

• Leave pesticides in their original containers; keep them tightly closed and make sure that the labels remain on them.

• Don't store pesticides near food or feed, under sink, in the pantry, in the medicine cabinet, or within reach of children and pets.

Pest Prevention

• Always practice good housekeeping; vacuum often and thoroughly.

• Follow good storage practices in the pantry; always use insect-proof containers.

• Buy food, even dog food, in small quantities rather than provide stored food for pests.

• Seal all entry points by plugging holes in house foundation, etc., be sure doors are tight fitting, that windows are screened.

• Don't have excess birdfeed in the yard or birdfeeder—it attracts rats and squirrels.

• Don't store firewood or anything against the house.

• Be careful of a compost pile; it's a great breeding ground for pests. Keep it far enough from your home so creeps won't come visiting.

• Use yellow patio lights and place them on the perimeter rather than on the house or patio; the perimeter lights will draw the bugs away.

How to Cope With Wet Basements

Though basements should be made watertight at the time of construction, water can occasionally appear even in the best built house, and a basement that is always damp or floods after a heavy rain is a real problem. While serious flooding will probably have to be handled by a mason or landscape contractor, there are a number of common conditions that you can easily deal with yourself.

Water enters a basement in three ways: leakage, seepage and condensation. Leakage is the main cause of large quantities of water and occurs because of either a simple crack in the wall, poor drainage or a high water table (the level of ground water in your area). You can easily locate obvious cracks in the wall and plug them with hydraulic cement, obtainable in most hardware or building-supply stores.

Water can also leak through cracks that are less easy to detect, or through the joint where the floor meets the walls, probably the result of poor drainage or a high water table. This can be corrected by regrading and sloping the ground away from the house (something best left to a landscaper unless you are a very energetic do-it-yourselfer).

Check downspouts from your gutters to make sure they're discharging water a good distance away from the foundation walls. (Keep gutters and downspouts free of debris. Where leaves and twigs from nearby trees can collect in a gutter, install a basket-shaped wire strainer over the downspout outlet.)

A waterproofing specialist may be needed for work on both the inside and the outside walls of the basement, or you may have to install a sump pump. This is a compact unit that fits into a pit in the low corner or wet spot of the basement. Designed for automatic operation, it is a pressure-relief system that raises the water to a level where it can be carried off through storm drains or other outside areas.

As a temporary solution, you can buy or rent a lightweight utility pump, which will remove as much as 1,300 gallons of water an hour from a flooded basement. Such pumps are small and easy to handle, relatively inexpensive, and can also be used to water lawns, drain or vacuum swimming pools and remove excess water from boats or other flooded places, such as lawns.

Seepage and condensation are conditions the homeowner can easily handle. (Both conditions may be occurring at the same time.) Mild seepage can be distinguished from condensation with a simple test: Tape a 12-inch square of aluminum foil on the damp wall, anchoring all four sides; make sure the bond is as airtight as possible. Leave it up a day or two; then remove. If the side of the foil that was against the wall is wet, seepage is occurring; if the side that faced out is wet, it's condensation.

Many seepage problems are created by water that collects along the foundations and seeps into the basement through old or cracked walls and floors. To prevent this, downspouts or gutters should be at least eight to ten feet from the foundations and directed into storm drains. Mild seepage can often be stopped with a good waterproofing paint or by repairing minor cracks in walls and floors with hydraulic cement. Severe seepage resembles leakage, with water trickling down the wall. First, try waterproofing paint on a section of the wall where seepage is occurring; you should be able to tell after a trial period whether the paint will help or not. If not, you may have to use the more extensive cures for leakage.

Condensation can occur when warm, moist air comes in contact with cool surfaces, such as cold-water pipes or masonry walls and floors. This can be eliminated by removing moisture from the air with a dehumidifier (it dries out the air before it can condense), by repairing leaky plumbing and by insulating all cold-water pipes. The basement should also be well ventilated and, if possible, have some sunlight. If there are trees and shrubbery planted around the basement, they should be trimmed and pruned away from the walls to allow for better light and air circulation.

Ladder Safety

A ladder is a household essential, needed to get up and at any number of housecleaning and decorating jobs. But if purchased thoughtlessly and used carelessly, a ladder can be a hazard instead of a help. Here we'll be talking about the 5- or 6-foot household stepladder and the typical kitchen step stool that a handyperson is most likely to be using indoors.

Forget about price when buying a stepladder; there's too much at stake to chance a rickety bargain. Look for a ladder that is sturdy and whose sections open to a wide spread—with a good locking device to keep that spread steady; strong steps that are level and uniformly spaced; and heavy, rustproof hardware that is firmly secured. During the life of a ladder, check it often for loose or missing screws and bolts, split steps, worn step treads, and worn-out caps at the base of the legs.

What to do if you find any of these unsafe conditions? Tighten screws and bolts and replace missing ones. If a step is badly weakened, repair it only if it is possible to restore the step to safe use; otherwise, invest in a new ladder. If a step edge is worn, the tread may be gone too, leaving nothing for your soles to grip; again, new treads, or a new ladder, are the answer.

Most step stools have caps on the ends of the legs. Metal or hard plastic caps may slide on waxed floors—so to keep things solid underfoot, replace them with rubber caps, which are available at hardware stores. Aluminum stepladders with rubber caps should be inspected frequently to make sure the metal legs are not forcing their way through the caps; if they are, get new ones that will fit as snugly as possible.

Wooden stepladders last longer if they're treated with two coats of clear varnish—not paint or lacquer, which conceal dangerous cracks and defects. Moving parts should be oiled about once a year. Aluminum ladders don't need a protective coating, although their moving parts should be kept lubricated.

How you use a stepladder is also important:

• Before climbing, make sure the braces on each side are down completely and locked firmly in place. A partially open stepladder may fold and collapse right from under you.

• Before you climb, make sure the soles of your shoes are not wet or greasy and that the steps are clean and dry. Be sensibly dressed—climbing in a long skirt and platform wedgies is just asking for trouble. And if you wear your hair long and loose, fasten it back.

• Don't stand on the top platform; it's best not to go higher than the second step from the top unless you've had training with Ringling Brothers.

• The folding platform that holds supplies and tools should be used only for that purpose, never as another place for you to stand on.

• Don't work on a ladder if your pockets are crammed with tools—put everything you need in a tool chest or basket and place it on the folding platform.

Don't attempt to reach farther than a comfortable arm's length away; it's safer to climb down and move the ladder. But don't try to move it while supplies and tools are on the folding platform.

• If you're working in or near a doorway, either lock the door shut or secure it in a fully open position so that others can't come smashing into it and send you toppling.

• If possible, place the ladder so that you can work facing toward it, not away from it. Don't ever climb down when facing away from the ladder.

• Store the ladder indoors on sturdy hangers, away from the floor. Keep wooden ladders away from excessive heat or dampness.

A New Look
for Old Marble

If the once-lustrous marble surfaces in your home are becoming a dingy shadow of their former selves, don't despair. There are ways to make things glow again.

Day-to-day maintenance is simple: Wipe marble surfaces with warm water, which may be fortified with a detergent solution if you wish. Act quickly after spills, though; marble, being somewhat porous, is vulnerable to damage from whatever troublemakers come in contact with it. And if the marble has been badly soiled or scarred by neglect or an accident, there are special rejuvenating procedures to take.

Etch Marks

These are caused by the acidic influence of wine, beer, fruit juice, vinegar, tomato products, mustard, carbonated beverages, ink or salad dressing. Some of these offenders will etch the finish with dull scuff marks, yet not leave a stain; others both etch and stain the polished finish. The remedy for a marred surface is a good rubdown with a marble-polishing powder, such as tin oxide, which is available in hardware stores, local marble shops or in special marble-care kits. Wet the surface with clear water; sprinkle on polishing powder and rub it into the marble with a damp cloth. Continue the massage until etch marks disappear and the surface shines.

Deep-Seated Stains

Deep stains call for the application of a poultice. Poultices are of two types: white blotting paper, white paper napkins or white cleansing tissues soaked in a special solution; and whiting or talc (your hardware store will have it) mixed with a solution into a thick, plaster-like paste. The solution varies, depending on the stain involved.

Organic stains are those caused by such things as tea, coffee, some cosmetics, wine, fruit and tobacco. Wash the surface with clean water and apply a poultice soaked with hydrogen peroxide (hair-bleaching strength) or full-strength household ammonia. Cover the poultice with a piece of glass or plastic to keep it from evaporating. This process of drawing the stain out of the marble may take from one to 48 hours, depending on how serious the problem is. Use rubber gloves, and take care.

Oil stains: Caused by butter, milk, cream, salad oils, peanut butter, mustard, crayons, hand cream, and the like, these stains usually have a very dark center that diffuses outward to a light halo. Use a poultice soaked in amyl acetate or acetone—available at your hardware store. Let the poultice dry. Then remove, and repeat if necessary. Rinse thoroughly.

Rust stains: Orange to brown in color, they are caused by flowerpots, nails, bolts and screws, cans, steel wool, certain types of soil, and so on. Use a poultice soaked in commercial iron-rust remover and kept moist until you get results; rinse clear with water. The marble's sheen is usually dulled or etched by this treatment, so follow with the polishing-powder routine.

Paint stains: Carefully use a razor blade or knife edge to remove as much paint as possible. Follow up with a poultice made with paint remover and take it off when dry. Bleach any remaining stain with a hydrogen-peroxide poultice. Keep it moist until it works. Rinse thoroughly after each application.

A piece of marble grown shabby from neglect can be spruced up considerably. After dealing with the emergencies we mention, avoid future tragedy by using a marble-sealer—it's an aid that helps protect the surface. Also available is a variety of cleaners, detergents, polishes, powders and sealers made especially for routine marble care and restoration. Some essentials even come in kits (one for $5.50 is available from the Marble Institute of America—their address is 1984 Chain Bridge Road, McLean, Virginia 22101).

There's a limit, however, to what can be accomplished at home. Marble that's been severely damaged, or ravaged by discoloration and surface wear and tear, may not respond to the above remedies; if so, don't lose your marbles—instead, consult a reputable dealer for professional service. Check the Yellow Pages of your phone book under "Marble," or write to the Marble Institute of America for their listing of experts in your area.

Hanging Things

You can hang almost anything on any sort of wall or ceiling if you know what kind of walls you have, which fasteners you need, and what tools to use.

There are two kinds of walls: hollow, which means there is open space between finished layers of interior and exterior surfaces; and solid—brick, stone, cement, cinder block—masonry all the way through. In most single family homes, the walls are hollow except for the basement. In apartment buildings, exterior walls and walls between apartments are solid, the rest hollow.

Which fasteners to use for what and where? Follow these clues:

To hang *heavy* things, such as big mirrors, large pictures, plants, mobiles, shelves, lighting fixtures, record and stereo cabinets on *hollow* walls, use the toggle (sometimes called Wing).

Toggle

A toggle works by opening its wings inside the wall, creating an anchor as its bolt is tightened from the front. It needs a big hole to get the folded wings through—use an electric or hand drill to predrill the hole. Toggles hold heavy loads more reliably than other fasteners and are just about the only thing to use when hanging things from the ceiling. (Weighty chandeliers should be put up by professionals.) They come in many sizes for thin or thick walls.

You can also use a Molly on *hollow* walls.

Molly

This works by forcing the split metal sleeves outward and up against the back of the inside of the wall when its bolt is tightened from the outside. The hole must be predrilled and must be the same size as the sleeve. The largest Molly is only 3 inches long so it won't work for very thick walls (use toggle instead). Mollies work well on walls surfaced with ceramic tile—predrill hole with carbide-tipped drill bit.

To hang *medium weights,* such as shelf standards, towel bars, shower rods, lamps, mirrors, pictures, clocks, ordinary curtain and drapery rods on *hollow or solid walls,* use plastic or fiber shields (sometimes called plugs or anchors).

Plastic or Fiber Shields

These work by gripping the sides of the hole they're in when a matching screw is driven in. Predrill a hole the same diameter as the shield and a tiny bit longer. They are ideal for mounting towel bars on hollow wood doors and work well on walls surfaced with ceramic tile.

To hang *heavy* things such as garden tools, storage cabinets and shelves, lighting fixtures, art objects, plant brackets on *solid* walls, use lead shields with screws.

Lead Shields with Screws

These work by expanding inside a pre-drilled hole; use electric drill with carbide-tipped bit or hammer and star drill. Hole must be the same diameter as the shield but slightly longer than the screw. Handy for mounting things on foundation walls, inside or out.

To hang *medium to lightweight* plant holders, shelves, lamps, mirrors, pictures and utensils on *solid walls* you can also use masonry nails, sometimes called cut nails.

Masonry Nails

These are tapered and grooved to cling to the solid material into which they are driven. You'll need a heavy hammer, and safety goggles would be a wise precaution. On exposed stone or brick walls, drive the nail into the mortar between the stones or brick.

To hang *heavy to medium weight* pictures, brackets, tools, lamps, etc., on *wood* doors, window frames and wall studs, use a simple wood screw.

Wood Screw

A bit of soap on the threads of the screw will make driving easier.

To hang *medium weight* curtain and drapery rods, shutters, shades and blinds, metal and glass plant shelves on *metal* doors, window frames and wall studs, use self-tapping sheet metal screws.

Sheet Metal Screws

These work by cutting their own threads, so to speak, as they move through the metal. Dent the metal surface you're going to drill through with a nail or nail setter. Use an electric drill with high speed steel bit to predrill a hole slightly smaller than the screw. Put a drop of oil on the drill bit. Half way through, remove drill, work oil into hole, and finish drilling.

Running Out of Space? Just Add a Room

At some point most families need more room, and the usual solution is to sell the current house and move to a larger one. But with the skyrocketing cost of new housing, plus the scarcity and high rates of mortgage money, this has become more difficult. The next best solution is to expand your present home; this will not only solve your space problem, but should add as much to the value of the house as the cost of the remodeling. Unlike mortgage loans, home-improvement loans are easy to acquire; in fact, banks promote them even as mortgage money remains in short supply.

There are many ways to add a room. Depending on the type of house and the space around it, on whether you build up or out and sometimes on local regulations, space may be found by enclosing a carport, a sun porch, a front porch or a second-floor porch; by converting a garage or building a room over a garage; by raising the attic roof; adding a loft room; converting a basement; or simply by extending the house with an addition.

Structural costs vary widely. For example: Adding a small dormer to extend the attic could cost less than $1,000; an extension to the back or side of the house, about $6,000 to $9,000; a loft extension from the roof, about $10,000; two bedrooms and bath over a two-car garage, as much as $15,000 to $20,000. Before launching into the project know exactly what's involved.

An extra room can be added quite easily to the back of a ranch house and be perfectly proportioned to it.

How to Begin

Once the purpose of the new space has been decided, let's say a bedroom and bath, certain preliminary investigations are necessary. Learn from your local building and zoning departments about any local regulations (zoning rules, building codes) that may limit the size of the expansion and where it can be placed. Zoning rules include setback requirements that specify how far the house must be from the street and property lines; these limits also apply to additions and could vary in different parts of town. Building codes deal with structural considerations, such as framing-lumber sizes, construction methods and foundation materials. Some codes may limit room sizes, window areas, and so on.

Early in the planning consider these points:

1. The location of the septic tank and drainage fields for homes so equipped. Since you can't build over the tank or field, or within the code-specified distance from them, this is an important consideration. If you don't already know the locations, look for the point where the largest plumbing pipes pass outward through basement wall or floor.

2. Plumbing. If the existing plumbing runs through a wall that will be altered or removed, expensive rerouting of plumbing could result.

3. Wiring. Again, wall alterations could necessitate expensive wiring changes.

4. Heating. Determine whether your present system can handle the additional load or whether a larger unit may be required. Modern insulation, along with your present heating system, can sometimes solve the problem.

5. Walls. Whether a particular wall can be removed depends on whether or not it is a load-bearing wall. If the wall supports the floor or structure above it, substitute support would have to be provided. If you wish, much of this preliminary investigation can be handled by the contractor.

In addition, major structural considerations may determine which route you take. For example, converting part of the basement into a recreation room may simply involve the addition of partition walls with studs, added insulation in the surrounding outside walls and some interior finishing, and might cost as little as $2,000. Converting a two-car garage to a bedroom and bath, perhaps involving floor, wall and ceiling finishing, heating, and so forth, could go as high as $5,000.

Other considerations:

• In raising a roof, old rafters will have to be removed, new rafters installed, new joists (small timbers or metal beams that support a floor or ceiling) and studs (wooden uprights in the framing of walls) to support a floor or ceiling may have to be added.

• Girders (horizontal main structural members) may be required to support vertical loads and rafters.

• Steel posts may be necessary to support a steel girder if weight load of the room requires it.

• If room is to be an extension of the house, a foundation, usually as much as 36 inches below frost line, must be dug. This is decided by the building inspector.

- For an extension to the back or side of house, a bearing beam must be installed across the top at the point where extension is added to the home. The size of this beam depends on the size of the extension. A double beam or stud may be required at the sides where the extension is added. Again, all is determined by the buiilding code.

- New subflooring, joists and bracing may be required in adding a room over a porch or garage. The floor joists may have to be doubled between garage and the add-on.

- You must also be sure the footing below the garage is able to hold the weight load of a second level.

- Because asbestos roofing shingles are heavier than asphalt ones, if you are considering switching from asphalt to asbestos, heavier (two-by-eights) roof rafters will be required.

- If brick siding is to be used, foundation wall must be wider to support the load.

- If paneling a concrete-wall basement, two-by-four studs must be put up on the wall and insulation stapled between them before applying the paneling; insulation keeps you warm and reduces the fuel bill.

This unusual and interesting loft extends from the roof in rear of house and provides a small balcony and covered patio area as well as an extra room.

Getting It Done

Guidance from a professional is important. If you are unable to settle on a plan of your own, or if special problems exist, an architect should be called in. He can act as a consultant only, presenting you with the best possible solution to your space problem at the lowest possible cost. Or, if you want professional supervision while the job is being done, the architect will work directly with the contractor. The architect will even select the contractor if you wish. An architect's fee is usually based on a percentage of the total remodeling costs. This fee will vary with the size and complexity of the project, but usually ranges from 15 to 25 percent. To select an architect, contact the local chapter of the American Institute of Architects or check the Yellow Pages of the phone book. Ask to see some previous work, and contact some of his clients for an appraisal of his ability.

If you decide to go directly to a contractor, consult friends, neighbors and relatives for recommendations of contractors with whom they have worked. Learn how long the contractor took to complete the job, what his charges were and the quality of his work. A local building-material dealer or building-supply yard owner might also be helpful. Still other sources are banks that specialize in home-improvement loans, the local remodelers' association, the Chamber of Commerce or Better Business Bureau. The contractor's reliability is more important than price, since he will be making major decisions for you throughout the project. When you have the names of several contractors, visit their showrooms or offices; be sure there is a permanent location and evidence of a healthy business. Get bids from at least three contractors after having given each the same requirements. Don't necessarily take the lowest bid—it may be low because they're leaving something out. For example, there would be a price difference between using insulating sheathing or fiber-glass insulation to close in an outer wall. In this regard, it's helpful to designate your own brands, specifying model or type; when restricted to one floor material, window type, wall paneling and the like, contractors' bids can be compared more easily.

Once the contractor has been selected, a contract is signed. This includes the price you've agreed on, the specifications and the plan. Go over these carefully; be sure the contract spells out exactly what will be done, how it will be done, the specific materials that will be used, the completion date and the payment schedule. If any change is made after the job gets under way, this should also be in writing with any cost changes included.

Do It Yourself?

There is great satisfaction in completing home-improvement projects yourself, but stick to what you really know how to do. Some projects require tradesmanlike skills; mistakes could be costly. With several subcontractors—electrician, plumber, mason, carpenter—coordinating everything could be a full-time job. Unless you have the time, the patience and the know-how, better leave this to the professional. His experience in purchasing materials and his access to trade discounts can save you money.

There are, however, many areas in which you can save money on labor, one of the largest costs in any project. These include painting, laying floor tiles or carpet squares, staining unfinished doors, putting up prefinished paneling after the contractor has leveled and furred the walls, and installing shelving by yourself. But when deciding what jobs you will handle, face the reality of possible costly mistakes and of a longer completion time than if a contractor did them.

Paying for the Project

Most homeowners finance a major remodeling project through a bank or savings-and-loan association; these lenders often advance the money in installments, to be paid to the contractor as work progresses. Some lenders may insist on bonding to insure the job is completed. When a loan is essential, be sure your finances are in order. If you have heavy debts, pay these first. A major debt, such as monthly car payments, could affect the amount of money you can borrow. Go to a lender who knows you, where you have other banking services, where you've financed a car or had another loan. Take along the contractor's cost estimates; the bank or loan association will need these to act on your application.

Most contractors expect progress payments. This means a certain amount paid when the contract is signed, another when work begins, another when rough framing is completed and the final amount when the project is completed.

Living Through It

A certain degree of disarray, dirt and noise is inevitable and you'll just have to live with it; the project can take up to a month or more, and if you stay out of the way and don't ask a lot of questions, the work will get finished without delay. There are times, though, when you should speak up—if you think you see a mistake being made, tell the architect or contractor. Keep pets and children out of the way; don't borrow the workers' tools—and don't ask them to baby-sit while you run an errand!

An inexpensive dormer opens up an enclosed
attic to light and air and gains a brand-new bedroom.

Home-Improvement Materials

With the great diversity of materials on the market today, creating a tasteful and comfortable living environment is really quite easy. Paints mixed to your own specifications, fabrics and wallpaper in all manner of patterns, textures, colors and price ranges, and innumerable prefinished wall panelings from natural woods to man-made duplicates that look like the real thing make for exciting decorating. Things are happening in exterior siding, in flooring materials and their application and even in bathroom fixtures. Local building-materials retailers offer extensive home-improvement centers—browse, look, compare costs.

1. The outside. Exterior siding for your new addition is no problem at all. The great variety of wood-siding patterns available means an almost-perfect match can be made of the old and the new. The charm of wood is that it also blends extremely well with other materials, such as brick. You can get rough-sawed boards for a rambling ranch house or smooth bevel siding for the precise outline of a Colonial. And there's clapboard, horizontal bevel, flush tongue and groove, wide bevel, board and batten, vertical narrow channel, and so on. And because wood is a natural insulator, you could realize savings on annual heating and air-conditioning costs.

Other popular siding materials include vinyl and aluminum. Some, with wood-grain texturing, resemble the look of wood so closely you can hardly tell the difference. Vinyl's adaptability results in an infinite variety of colors, shapes, sizes and textures. It requires little if any maintenance and regular repainting is unnecessary; it resists chipping, peeling, flaking, scratching, rotting and denting. Aluminum siding similarly requires very little maintenance. Various chemically applied plastic coatings are used with it to provide protection and color, and the finish lasts for many years before painting is necessary.

2. Interior paneling. If you elect to panel the interior of your new room, there are many kinds of wood to choose from, each with its own characteristic look and unique grain and knot pattern, ranging from the familiar walnut, oak, birch, elm, pecan, cherry, and so on, to exotic imports. Select the paneling in natural hardwood or the less-expensive simulated woods. The former comes smooth-finished or rough-sawed for a rustic, informal effect. In addition to the natural look of hardwoods, many panels

have a factory-applied coloration that imparts a distinctive character to the face veneer; it might be antiquing, shadowing or plank tonings. Even pastel colors, such as blue, green, pink or yellow, are available to harmonize or contrast with furnishings or other walls. Though paneling is usually installed vertically, try it diagonally or horizontally or in combinations for a particularly interesting effect. Special finishes on some paneling make it impervious to smears, grease, and so on.

3. Floor coverings. Your new room's floor can be finished in a number of ways: resilient flooring either in tiles or sheet form, wood parquet blocks or carpeting. Floor tiles are of three basic materials: vinyl, asphalt and vinyl asbestos. Asphalt tile is the least expensive but has some drawbacks in durability and maintenance. Vinyl asbestos is moderately priced but a bit limited in styles. Vinyl is the top of the line, has good wear and maintenance qualities, patterns and colors, and can even simulate stone, brick and other unusual patterns. You can save money by laying tiles yourself—they come with easy-to-follow instructions.

Use wasted air space over a two-car garage to add
two bedrooms and a bath to this small Colonial.

Sheet vinyl also has good wear and maintenance qualities and when installed looks virtually seamless. Cushioned backing adds comfort to resilient flooring, and no-wax types are extremely easy to care for. To make a particularly attractive and coordinated decorating scheme, matching fabric and wall covering are available to team up with some vinyl cushioned flooring. Wood parquet blocks can be found in a variety of different woods and in several styles. They are either prefinished or ready to finish, and many have tongue-and-groove edges for rigid locking. Carpeting adds warmth and comfort to a room and softens noise. It runs the gamut of fibers from acrylic to wool, each with its own wear, resilience and care characteristics. Prices range from about $6 to $28 a square yard. Do-it-yourself carpet tiles with adhesive backing are easy to install. They come in shag and plush styles.

4. Ceilings. Ceiling treatment is an equally important part of the room. You can paint, paper, tile, even beam or panel it. Painting or papering is obviously the quickest and least expensive. A tile ceiling gives a room a smart contemporary look. Seamless installation is now possible and again skilled handypersons could save money by installing it themselves. Consider acoustical tiles, which help to create a quiet atmosphere; planks that look and feel like natural wood; and vinyl-coated tiles that are scrubbable and easy to care for. The gay deceivers—fake beams—can add a dramatic look to the room; vinyl beams on wood strips are simply nailed to the ceiling and foam beams are glued in place.

5. Bathrooms. If a bathroom is being added, here are some new things you should know about. Ceramic tile now comes in pregrouted sheets of one foot square to make application especially easy; there is even a packaged tub-surround, consisting of eight large sheets of tile, which will fit a standard 60-inch tub and extend 56 inches above the tub. New one-piece fiber-glass units are especially suited to remodeling projects; there are tub-shower units, shower stalls and an acrylic-surfaced fiber-glass tub. Also new are polyester-marble tubs that almost look like the real thing. Toilets, too, have a new look, with plastic being used for everything except the bowl, which is still china. The flushing handle of one unit has been replaced with a press tab at the corner, flush-mounted with the top of toilet tank.

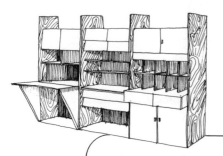

Finding Storage Space You Didn't Know You Had

The problem of storing all your possessions often seems insurmountable. Out-of-season clothing, records and documents, luggage, sewing supplies and equipment, folding table and chairs—where can they all fit? In fact, storage facilities often exist in space you never dreamed you had. Here are 56 ways to ease the storage squeeze:

• Give away things that haven't been used or worn in the last two years.

• Put infrequently used items on higher shelves or store them in the basement or attic.

• Make use of wasted closet space by adding extra shelves that can double or triple the closet's storage capacity. If possible, make the shelves adjustable. For most shelves, 18 inches should be the maximum depth; otherwise, things get lost.

• Create your own modular storage system with stackable storage boxes—the sturdier ones might go from floor to ceiling. Some are completely closed and pull out like a filing cabinet; others are open at the top to receive things like toys, magazines, records, etc.

• Sturdy cartons, wooden crates or plywood boxes make excellent storage units. Spray-paint or cover with adhesive-backed covering.

Bathroom

• Use wasted air space above bathroom fixtures by adding extra cabinets or shelves high on the wall. Vanity organizers that sit on top of the toilet tank store toiletries, as do pole organizers with open and closed shelves.

• Hang a shower caddy over the shower head, or place one in the corner of the tub to hold everything for a shower or shampoo.

• Utilize the empty cavity in the sink cabinet by adding shelves, either fitted around the pipes or along the sides, to hold extra tissues, soap, toothpaste, cleaning supplies.

• Use a hanging wine rack to hold rolled towels; it's not only useful but decorative and interesting.

• A folding hat rack "hangs" more towels than the usual towel bar.

• Small wood or glass shelves, one for each member of the family, make use of unused bathroom-wall space.

• The back of the bathroom door can be used for other than nightclothes; hang a small "soft" clothes hamper here, or a caddy or two to hold shavers, hair rollers, and so on.

Bedroom

• Make the bedroom closet more space-saving by the addition of partitions, shelves, boxes and double-tiered hanging rods for shirts, blouses, jackets and skirts. Make the shelves of various widths so things can be stored one deep—narrowest at the top, widest at the bottom. If there's room, built-in drawers are also useful.

• Elusive, unmanageable, space-stealing belts can be tamed in a number of ways: Improvise with a sturdy coat hanger, and loop and buckle the belts over the lower section; or attach a towel bar inside the closet door and loop as above. Special belt racks from which the belts individually hang by the buckle are available at notions counters.

• Empty suitcases offer an abundance of storage space: You can use them for blankets, out-of-season clothing, summer slip-covers and curtains or for extra linens. Or use under-bed storage boxes that can slide in and out easily.

• There are many space-saving ways to store shoes besides the familiar fabric or plastic bag on the back of a door. The original shoe boxes stack neatly on a closet floor up to hem level of the hung garments (identify each with a marking pen or a label). Plastic bags with closed pockets for each pair of shoes hang from the clothes rod. Compartment shoe boxes for shelf or floor hold several pairs; open cabinets divided into one-pair slots, or chests with see-through fronts hold many pairs. And of course there are the open shoe racks that men seem to prefer.

• Line up handbags on a shelf one deep (if used infrequently, you may want to cover them with a plastic sheet to keep the dust out). If you have the space in your closet, a hanging plastic bag with individual closed pockets is very convenient. Off-season bags go in empty suitcases or storage boxes.

• Hats are the best stored in their original boxes; mark each box and stack on closet shelf or put under the bed. Hatstands are convenient if you have lots of closet space.

• The space in bureau drawers can be much more efficiently utilized if you use wood, plastic or cardboard dividers to keep such things as scarves, ribbons, gloves, handkerchiefs and lingerie neatly separated. Accessory boxes are also available for this purpose, or make your own from gift boxes.

• Multiple skirt, blouse and trouser hangers will hold several in the space of one.

• Take advantage of plastic organizers that have stalls for lip-sticks and compartmented trays for cosmetics. Or make your own from small, shallow boxes.

• Space-saving jewelry storage can be accomplished in a shallow drawer by using lots of plastic dividers; gift boxes or accessory boxes might serve, too. If storing jewelry in a drawer, line drawer with a thin layer of foam rubber to keep the jewelry from getting mixed up.

• Use bookcases in a child's bedroom to separate play and sleep areas; put toys on one side, books and "possessions" on the sleeping side. Stackable cubes make excellent cubby-holes to house all the things children collect. Pegboard and hooks make good use of wall space as does a wall organizer with pockets.

• Drawers built under a bed are convenient for storing heavy clothing, blankets, sports equipment, and so on.

Living and Dining Room

• Add shelves or free-standing units such as étagères along a wall to store books, electronic equipment, collectors' items. Adjustable shelves can be arranged according to the size of the books.

• A hollow hassock doubles as storage space and footstool.

• A flat-top trunk makes an interesting coffee or end table, and it holds a lot.

• If there's no hall or closet for coats, put pegs on the wall or even up the stairs.

• Space-saving cushioned cases not only protect china and glassware but hold many similar things—cups and saucers, for instance—in little space.

• Sufficient long, shallow drawers for proper storage of table linens seldom exist—put linens in suit boxes under the sofa, or you can hang table linens on a wooden coat hanger.

• File cabinets that look just like pieces of furniture will serve as occasional tables and will hold family records, tax information and other valuable papers.

• Use a section of bookcases as a room divider when the front door enters directly into living room. Besides providing a great storage wall, it creates a hallway.

• Close in the space under a staircase leading to another floor to store folding chairs, folding bed, extra leaves of dining-room table, luggage.

• In some houses the upstairs hallway may present some interesting storage possibilities. An alcove or nook might be utilized for a desk, cabinet or closet.

Kitchen

• Add a kitchen island to gain more work and storage space; it might be an interesting piece of furniture purchased at a garage or tag sale.

• Add casters to a small table or cabinet that could slide under a counter; roll it out for arranging flowers, sewing, or when cooking.

• Install narrow shelves or cabinets in the space between counter top and bottom of wall cabinets to store spices, herbs and other small items within easy reach.

• One-can-deep shelving, behind a door, for instance, converts this space into a veritable pantry.

• Mount pegboard on wall or inside of cabinet or closet doors to hold a multitude of tools. Pretty decorative hooks will also serve.

• File hard-to-store food envelopes in a good-size plastic freezer container; or use an acrylic plastic cube.

• Spice racks will free precious storage space in wall cabinets.

• Slide-out drawers and vegetable bins make use of the wasted space under sink; a stacking kit creates two-level storage.

• Use turntables or lazy Susans on deep shelves or in corner cabinets.

• Adjustable shelves in cabinets make maximum use of the space but too few cabinets have them; in tall spaces use vinyl-covered metal stacking shelves for multilevel storage.

• Attach drawers beneath wall cabinets to store bread, kitchen wraps, paper towels and almost anything else you can't find room for.

• Utilize deep drawers to their fullest by dividing them vertically to store baking dishes, pan covers, bulky-kitchen tools. Fit shallow drawers with partitions or accessory trays to keep small things from rolling around.

Basement and Garage

• Basement stairwells offer found storage space for flower containers, canned and packaged foods, bulky roasters, seldom-used utensils. Use hooks, pegboard or shelves.

• Open metal shelf units provide organized storage for cartons of Christmas decorations, scrapbooks, picnic gear, fans, and so forth, and protect them from the dampness of the floor. Be sure cartons are well identified. Metal cabinets are a good place for extra canned goods, paint and painting equipment and workshop supplies.

• A cedar closet in the basement is a good place to keep out-of-season clothing.

• At the workbench, small metal and plastic cabinets with lots of mini drawers not only organize nails, nuts, bolts, and so on, but take up very little space. A tool caddy or discarded lunch pail keeps things together and can be easily moved for repair jobs throughout the house.

• Screw-top jars can be nailed by the top to underside of shelves to hold nails, screws, etc.

• Consider an outdoor prefab tool shed to house garden furniture, barbecue grill, extra tires, firewood and other big items.

• Garage walls offer endless storage possibilities; a pegboard will hold a vast amount of tools; shelves and cabinets will hold auto-repair and cleaning equipment, gardening supplies and the like.

• Use overhead space to store screens and storm windows, porch furniture, skis, fishing rods; place boards across the rafters to make a flat surface.

Closets

• Dedicate one closet in the house to the family miscellany that clutters up clothes closets. One half might be used for sports equipment, such as skates, skis, golf clubs, tennis rackets, basketballs, helmets, etc. With partitions and shelves of various sizes, the equipment could even be arranged according to the season. The other half, again properly sectioned, could house movie or slide projector, screen, slides, picnic and camping gear, musical instruments.

• Clean up the cleaning closet to get the best use of its cavernous space; use the walls and door for hanging; add shelves to organize the vast array of supplies; use special holders for ironing table and iron, vacuum-cleaner attachments and broom and dustpan; hang a shoe bag to hold cloths, sponges and smaller containers of cleaners.

A New Look
For
Laundry Areas

Where is the laundry done in your home? In a dark and gloomy basement? In the kitchen where clothes get in the way of food preparation? In some remote part of the house where you have to traipse back and forth in order to get the job done? If your laundry center is not in the most convenient location, you *can* do something to change this situation.

Remodeling is on the minds of many homeowners these days. If you're one of them, it's a good time to tackle the laundry problem. Laundries traditionally were located in the basement because it positioned the washer close to the outdoor clothes line. With the clothes line but a memory, with today's washable and dryable fabrics and with advances in laundry appliance technology, the laundry process has been simplified to the extent that a full-size laundry room may no longer be necessary. Instead, a compact laundry *area* may be all you need to achieve the utmost in convenience and efficiency.

A look around your home will probably suggest a number of locations. It might be a corner off the kitchen; a large closet with a stackable washer and dryer; a niche at the end of a second floor hall, near the bedrooms and bath where soiled clothes collect and where it is near to existing plumbing. Your laundry area might be under a stairway where there is usually unused space; or against a wall in guest room or den, neatly concealed by folding, sliding or louvred doors or screens; or even in a dressing room or bathroom.

One thing to beware of: If your washer is upstairs, and if it overflows for some reason, the water damage could be considerable. As you plan, keep plumbing and utility connections in mind; an ideal location would be an area where the utilities can be shared with the present kitchen or bath. Plan the space requirements carefully; a washer and dryer placed side by side may require as little as 53 inches of space or as much as 58 inches. Depending on type, number and size of storage units used around the appliances, the area could be quite compact.

The laundry area doesn't have to be fancy, but should be designed to contain everything you need. Besides the washer and dryer, a few simple shelves, either open or closed, may be built along the sides and over the top of appliances to hold laundry aids such as detergent, bleach, fabric softener, pretreatment product, stain removal supplies, etc. "Milk carton" cubes that you can buy in any department store in an array of colors may be stacked and arranged around the appliances. Simple but sturdy boxes or crates, covered with colorful adhesive-backed decorative paper or painted in pretty colors, may add the desired storage space—arrange them as you wish. One thing to remember is that if there are small children in the house you should keep cleaning supplies out of their reach, so it's best to put these on the higher shelves. If you buy detergent by the tub you'll want it in a low space for most convenient use; if there are small children around close off and lock this storage space. Keep a supply for current use on a higher shelf and replenish the detergent as needed.

Some kind of roll-out bin for collection of soiled clothes, perhaps for delivery of folded clean clothes later, would be handy to stash under a counter next to the washer and dryer. Or include a few pull-out bins or drawers if there's space, for the assortment of collectibles and deliverables. A couple of wall cabinets, one of them locked, may be useful. Wall cabinets should be low enough so you can easily reach shelves on which frequently used items are stored, but out of reach of children. If wall cabinets are directly above washer, be sure to allow for clearance of opened washer lid. If there is no space for even a narrow base cabinet which also provides counter surface, tops of appliances may be used as work area.

Wherever you place the laundry area, be sure it allows for easy access to water and drain connections, and permits the dryer to exhaust to the outside. An electric dryer will require a separate 3-wire, 230-volt, 30-amp circuit. A gas dryer needs easy access for connections to the gas supply line; it also requires a 115-volt connection for its motor.

Though much ironing has been eliminated with today's fabrics, there are a few times when some ironing or pressing is required. The ironing table might be stored in a full-length closet nearby. If there is no closet, store the ironing table in a narrow slot between the appliances and wall; iron and ironing aids could fit nicely on a nearby shelf.

The laundry area should be located in the basement only when no other choice is feasible. Studies have shown that an upstairs location can reduce footsteps by as much as one half. Also, today's modern laundry appliances, with their attractive styling and colors, needn't be hidden away in the basement. If your laundry must be in the basement, set it off and pretty up the area surrounding it with previously mentioned solutions, plus some interesting wall treatment and camouflaging of exposed pipes.

adhesives, 6, 14-16
air conditioner maintenance, 50
alcohol spots, 89
aluminum discoloration, in the
dishwasher, 55

Index